For Megan.

Without you, none of this would be possible.

I0461187

"Keep Stacking Games" seemed to be the internal Thunder team motto. Hardly an interview went by without a Thunder player or coach blandly deflecting a question with "we just keep stacking days", or "stacking games", or "stacking wins."

It was (and is) an integral part of Coach Daigneault's culture. The coaches expected the players to improve every single day, no matter how good they were. Small improvements would add up over time. But his bigger point was to never be satisfied, and to keep moving forward. Keep stacking days.

It was also a reminder not to get too high or too low about individual games. Coach Daigneault expected players to learn from a bad loss, improve, and move forward. The expectation was that results would be better next time.

The Thunder also did not look ahead to big, upcoming games. Their focus remained on that day's practice or that day's game, nothing more. A long winning streak was seen as a one-game winning streak or, more likely, a zero-game winning streak. All that mattered was the next thing in front of them.

When the next game was all that mattered, full effort was expected, and given, every single night. The secret to the Thunder's success was spelled out

Keep Stacking Games:

The 2025 OKC

Championship Season

By Brian Benanzer

in every one of their boring, monotonous interviews:

Keep stacking games.

Prologue

Everyone knew this Oklahoma City team would be really good in 2025, but would they be good enough to win it all? It became clear at some point in the season that they were that good. But it was a long journey- they played over 100 games in the 2024/25 season. The events started running together for me.

As the playoffs started, I found myself trying to remember it all. I didn't want to misremember or guess at what had transpired, so I kept researching to remind myself exactly how the season went down. Games get blurred and the facts get forgotten.

Do you remember Chet Holmgren's hot start to the year? I didn't. He was the talk of the team at the beginning of the year- the lottery pick coming good with an All-Star level of play on the offensive and defensive ends. What about the Cleveland Cavaliers? They started out the season by winning their first 15 games. Their dominance was the talk of the league, and they had the NBA's best record for much of the year. What about when OKC was forced to start Jalen Williams at center for five straight games? Our 6'6" small forward was the tallest player on the court for much of those contests, as Chet, J-Will, and Hartenstein were all hurt. He put in a valiant effort, but not having a true big man didn't go well for the Thunder.

Additionally, THIS particular Thunder team, in addition to being so talented on the court, were also so damn lovable. Just a perfect team of selfless individuals, dedicated to their task and happy for each other's successes. And they almost never took a game off, which was about impossible during an 82-game NBA season. The Russ and KD era Thunder teams took nights off all the time, and the most games they ever won in a season was 60. The 2025 team played hard every night, a hallmark of the Thunder since Coach Daigneault took over.

Sam Presti said it way better than I have here. "The players from this team, they will be immortalized, not because they delivered a trophy to Oklahoma, but because they did so in a fashion that everyone in this state can easily relate to and understand. And that is their greatest legacy."

In professional sports, it's rare to see a group bond like this. They played true team basketball, all while handling life's pressures and their careers. Things will start changing with this group as they grow older, and some players will have to leave. The 2025 Thunder were unique- I don't see how a team can be more special than this one was.

I decided to endeavor on this project because I figured I'm not the only one who wants to remember it all, but can't. THIS Thunder team deserves to be celebrated in print. This was my love letter to them.

Glossary of Nicknames

Brad, Jay, and Jeff- They are three of my best friends, and they make appearances in the book. I include some of our text thread to remember how we felt about the team at different moments of the season. We also attended many games together. Brad has had Thunder season tickets since 2008.

The Thunder players had nicknames, as any good sports team would. Unfortunately, I was not privy to what most of them were. But my friends and I made plenty of our own nicknames for them and other NBA players. I hope it won't be too confusing for my readers, but I will persist in using my nicknames.

Sam Presti created an immediate problem when he drafted Jalen Williams and Jaylin Williams back-to-back in 2022. How would anyone be able to tell their names apart? Would they be called Cali Jalen and Arkansas Jaylin? Jay with an E and Jay with an I? An inspired Thunder broadcast team differentiated them with J-Dub and J-Will, and those nicknames stuck.

Shai Gilgeous-Alexander was a ridiculously long name for someone who was part of every Thunder conversation. In Oklahoma, he was known as Shai or SGA. But I prefer my own creation, Gil Goose, which was almost his name, plus no one has had the nickname "Goose" since Top Gun in 1986. I love it. I'm sticking with it. I invite you to use it too.

Thunder players nicknames...

Gil Goose- Shai Gilgeous-Alexander

J-Dub- Jalen Williams (from California)

J-Will- Jaylin Williams (from Arkansas)

Frankenstein- Isaiah Hartenstein

AC- Alex Caruso

Other NBA Players Nicknames...

Johnny Boy- Giannis Antetokounmpo of the Milwaukee Bucks.

Boy George- Paul George of the Philadelphia 76ers.

Luka the Fat- Luka Doncic of the LA Lakers (and Dallas Mavs).

Wemby- Victor Wembanyama of the San Antonio Spurs.

Cousin of Goose- Nickeil Alexander-Walker of the Minnesota Wolves.

J-Butts- Jimmy Butler of the Golden State Warriors.

Karlton- Karl Anthony Towns of the New York Knicks.

Thibs- Tom Thibodeau, Head Coach of the New York Knicks.

JJJ- Jaren Jackson Jr of the Memphis Grizzlies.

Turd Ferguson- Terrance Ferguson, former Thunder player (and Norm McDonald's nickname for Burt Reynolds on Saturday Night Live's Celebrity Jeopardy).

Contents

The 2025 Regular Season

How did the OKC Thunder players arrive onto the team? It was a quick roster rebuild after trading Russell Westbrook and Paul George in 2019.

2019

- Gil Goose (trade for Boy George)
- Lu Dort (Undrafted Free Agent)

2020

- Kenrich Williams (trade for Steven Adams)

2021

- Josh Giddey (1st round, 6th pick)
- Aaron Wiggins (2nd round, 55th pick)

2022

- Chet Holmgren (1st round, 2nd pick)
- Jalen Williams (1st round, 12th pick)
- Jaylin Williams (2nd round, 34th pick)
- Isaiah Joe (Free Agent)

2023

- Cason Wallace (1st round, 10th pick)

2024

- Isaiah Hartenstein (Free Agent)
- Alex Caruso (trade for Josh Giddey)
- Ajay Mitchell (2nd round, 58th pick)

To summarize this Sam Presti masterclass on how to build a championship team, the Thunder capitalized on overlooked players (Kenrich Williams, Isaiah Joe). Presti made a couple of great trades (SGA, Caruso), and he enticed a big free agent to come (Hartenstein). Presti also convinced an undrafted player to sign (Dort). Finally, he hit the jackpot on lottery picks (Chet Holmgren, Jalen Williams, Josh Giddey, Cason Wallace), and he also hit big on 2nd round picks (Aaron Wiggins, Jaylin Williams, Ajay Mitchell).

Of course, it wasn't flawless. Aleksej Pokusevski (2020) and Ousmane Dieng (2022) were both 1st round picks, and I was still unsure they knew how to play basketball above a high school level. And Presti had traded multiple 1st round picks to move up to draft them. The Thunder had drafted Alperen Sengun in 2021, and then immediately traded him away. He was already an All-Star. Other picks that missed included Tre Mann (2021-1st), Keyonte Johnson (2023-2nd), and Dillon Jones (2024-1st).

Some luck, of course, also was involved. And the players have worked so hard to improve themselves. Nobody foresaw Gil Goose or J-Dub developing into superstars that could lead their team to a championship. But it was also important that half of the team's rotation players came from castoffs that all the other NBA teams didn't want at all.

Oct 24th in Denver. Win vs Nuggets 102-87.

The season started against Denver, one of the league's best teams, and winners of 133 games and an NBA Championship over the previous two seasons. Jaylin Williams pulled his hamstring and Isaiah Hartenstein broke his wrist in the preseason, so the Thunder played a nine-man rotation. Isaiah Joe started alongside the four locked-in-pen starters: Gil Goose, J-Dub, Dort, and Chet. Cason Wallace, Aaron Wiggins, and Alex Caruso came off the bench with Ousmane Dieng. 2nd round pick Ajay Mitchell also played 7 minutes. This was surprising, because nothing was expected of him this season with the team this deep.

The Thunder had a 7-point lead at halftime. In what would become normal for this team, OKC went on a 18-2 run in the 3rd quarter. The killer blow for the Nuggets happened with 3 minutes to go. Nikola Jokic went up for a layup, but he was stuffed by Chet. Cason Wallace started a fast break, and passed the ball to Goose. Goose dropped a bounce pass into the lane for Chet, who streamed in for a dunk. The Thunder led by 17 going into the 4th quarter, and they cruised to an opening night victory.

A recurring theme this season would be elite guards experiencing really bad nights against

OKC's suffocating defense. Jokic had a triple double, as usual, but Jamal Murray was Dorted, with only 12 points on 4-of-13 shooting in 38 minutes. It was a very promising win in a tough place to play to start the season.

Oct 26th in Chicago. Win vs Bulls 114-95.

Coach Daigneault switched up his starting lineup, inserting Cason Wallace in place of Isaiah Joe. Daigneault would spend the first months of the season interchanging Wiggins, Wallace, and Joe in the lineup, trying to figure out who to start permanently. Ajay Mitchell also played 16 minutes, although it wasn't much of a game. The Thunder used a 22-to-3 run in the 2nd quarter to go up 59-39 at halftime, and easily won. And Alex Caruso received a well-deserved standing ovation from the Chicago fans after playing for them for the past 3 years.

Alex Caruso

2024 was a surprisingly excellent season for such a young Thunder team, but it ended very disappointingly in a crushing playoff series against Dallas. The Mavericks had made it very obvious that this Thunder team was missing some pieces to contend for a title. Could OKC grow into a championship-winning team? They would improve, but the championship window was already starting to close despite just being opened in 2024.

After the Dallas debacle, Sam Presti had traded for Alex Caruso. Presti hoped Caruso would bridge the gap to becoming a title contender. I have never heard anyone utter a bad word about OKC for making this trade. And I don't think the Bulls were out of line, either, as Caruso was going to be a free agent in one more year. Josh Giddey, whom they got in return, was really talented.

But Caruso.... Wow. Everybody following the Thunder was excited about his addition. I expected him to immediately become my favorite player. Caruso was a very smart athlete. He offered nearly every basketball skill to a team, and did them all well. Beyond Caruso's general competence on the basketball court, his individual defense was relentless. He was like a pit bull when attacking an opponent with the ball, snipping here and there, and coming back for more. Over and over. Again and again. The energy required to play like Caruso was substantial. He never took a moment off. It was an exhausting way to play. Few players could do it.

And how exhausting it was to play against him! Typically, players were allowed to slowly dribble up the court while taking in the defense. They could set the play, direct traffic, and catch their breath before attacking. But not against Caruso. His pressure began before the ball was ever received. He left no time for his opponent to think, much less set a play or run an offense. Playing against him was just survival. To successfully pass the ball off to a teammate was a win.

Caruso's story was an American dream, a rise from nothing to the top of the NBA. By twist of fate, he had started his professional basketball career playing for Coach Daigneault. They were on the Thunder's development league team together. Coach Daigneault remembered Caruso during that year "controlling the huddles. He was the voice." Years ago, Presti told Caruso's Oklahoma City Blue team what Presti wanted in a Thunder player. "A guy you don't have to worry about off the court, a great teammate, a guy who can defend multiple positions." He might as well have been describing Caruso exactly.

Caruso left Oklahoma City in 2017 to sign a 2-way contract with the Lakers, and he slowly forced his way into their team. In 2018 and 2019 he played 62 total games for Los Angeles. By 2020, he was a very important rotation member for what would be a championship team. Caruso shined especially brightly in the playoffs for the Lakers.

After the Lakers' 2021 title defense ended in disappointment due to injuries to LeBron James and Anthony Davis, their de-facto GM LeBron decided to make some changes. His championship teammates Kyle Kuzma and Kentavious Caldwell-Pope were traded for Russell Westbrook. Then

Caruso was released as a free agent so LA could re-sign the forgettable Talen Horton-Tucker. LeBron also had his old friend (and I mean OLD) Carmelo Anthony signed to his Los Angeles team.

The Lakers had now revamped their championship-winning defense led by Caruso and KCP into one featuring Russ and Carmelo instead. The combination of an old Russ and an old Carmelo had already completely failed for the Oklahoma City Thunder. And that was in 2018. To no one's surprise, except maybe LeBron's, that same combination also didn't work for the Lakers four years later. Los Angeles would finish with a losing record in 2022 and miss the playoffs again.

LA's loss was the Chicago Bulls gain. Chicago jumped at the chance to sign Caruso to a very reasonable 4-year/$37 million contract, and he rewarded them for it. He missed much of his first season in Chicago after Grayson Allen fractured his wrist with a cheap flagrant foul. Over his next two years, Caruso was honored for his excellent defense with an NBA All-Defense 1st team award in 2023 and an All-Defense 2nd team in 2024.

It didn't take long for Alex Caruso to prove his worth to the Thunder, either. Sam Presti offered his former D-League player a contract extension of 4-years/$81 million not long after trading for him. 2025 was an odd year for Caruso, because the

Thunder treated him with kid gloves. They held him out of many games and limited his minutes all season long. OKC had so many young players who needed to develop, unlike the 31-year-old Caruso. They had acquired him for the playoffs, not for the regular season.

With such a deep team, I spent the summer wondering who would be in Coach Daigneault's crunch-time playoff lineup? There were so many possibilities. Gil Goose and J-Dub obviously would be there, but whoever else it ended up being, I was sure that Caruso would be included as well.

Alex Caruso was a player who never should have made it. He overachieved through hard work and perseverance, and stayed humble while doing it. Every Oklahoman liked to envision himself also possessing those characteristics. And we loved Caruso for it. Could a player earn a statue in front of the stadium after just one season while playing only 19 minutes a game? Caruso might have done just that.

Oct 27th in OKC. Win vs Atlanta 128-104.

The Oklahoma City crowd was rocking for the home opener, but the Hawks played this one tough. Atlanta led by a point at halftime, and they led 91-92 in the 4th quarter. The Thunder then stole the game away with a 13-to-0 run. The Thunder went 14-of-23 from the field in the 4th quarter, while Atlanta shot just 6-of-20. Gil Goose dominated the contest with an amazing stat line of 35 points, 11 rebounds, 9 assists, 3 steals, and 3 blocks.

Oct 30th in OKC. Win vs Spurs 105-93.

Although it ended up being a close game, the Thunder had a 15-point lead at halftime. But the lead shrunk to 12 at the end of the 3rd quarter, and down to 7 in the 4th at 82-75. OKC then went on a 9-2 run to put the game away. Ajay Mitchell led the way, scoring five points while drawing a charge and adding a steal and a rebound.

Ajay Mitchell

Ajay Mitchell had come out of nowhere for the Thunder, and the rich had gotten richer. He was a 23-year-old rookie, born during the same week as J-Dub. Mitchell was Belgian, which made me speculate that Presti would stash Ajay in Europe. This would save a roster spot for somebody else. But Presti wanted Ajay Mitchell on his team. And he was willing to make a trade during the draft to get him (somehow OKC didn't have one of their 700 2nd round picks available in 2024).

It turned out that Ajay was a really good player. He earned a spot in the rotation during training camp despite the talent already in the Thunder lineup. Mitchell did not have a DNP- Coach's Decision all season. He could shoot 3's (38% in

2025) and was good off the dribble. He also wasn't afraid to take it to the hoop every play, similar to Aaron Wiggins. Ajay was better offensively than Cason Wallace in 2025 in my opinion (keep in mind that Cason was younger than Mitchell. I also think Cason was going to have a big, big year in 2026). Ajay scored in double-figures 11 times his rookie season despite missing over half of the games. He was the exact type of talented bench player that Denver and Milwaukee wished they had. And what did the Thunder have to give up to get him? Lindy Waters, an undrafted player that OKC had developed during the recent lean years. Waters wasn't in the Thunder's future plans at all.

Unfortunately, Ajay's 2025 season got cut short after surgery on his toe after his 34th game. Ajay did return from his injury for the last two games of the regular season, but he didn't have enough time to integrate back into the rotation before the playoffs. He ended up playing in 12 of the 23 playoff games, but most of his minutes were in garbage time.

2026 will be a big one for Ajay. He already had been moved from a 2-way contract to a full NBA deal. Then, after the 2025 season, he was signed to a 3 year/ $9 million contract. The Thunder's management team rated him, and the coaching staff was impressed by him. But the Thunder was already loaded with guards, and now Nikola Topic will be coming in for his rookie season. Ajay will have to earn his minutes all over again in 2026. But his performances this past year had him looking like his future was bright.

Nov 1st in Portland. Win vs Blazers 137-114.

Coach Daigneault spread the play time around for the second straight game, as ten guys played between 17 and 29 minutes each. Although the Blazers were expected to be bad (and they indeed ended up sucking in 2025), this game was up and down. The Thunder jumped out to a 13-point lead after the 1st quarter, but Portland bounced back to tie the score heading into halftime. The Thunder then scored 19 points off of 12 Blazer turnovers in the 3rd quarter to go up by 21. Chet was in foul trouble and only played 18 minutes, but he still managed to record 5 blocks.

I was already really excited about this team although the season had just begun. I texted my friends that the Celtics were the only other team on the same level as the Thunder. Brad pointed out that the Cavs were also really good. The Thunder defense was playing so well, and their best defender was always Brad's favorite player. I asked him how he would pick with so many choices this year?

5 Thunder games. 5 Thunder wins.

Nov 2nd in LA. Win vs Clippers 105-92.

The game was close, and Coach Daigneault shortened the rotation to basically 8 players. Wiggins started for the first time this season, alongside Goose, Dort, Chet, and J-Dub. Caruso, Cason, and Joe came off the bench. The Thunder was still without J-Will, Frankenstein, and Kenrich Williams, so the rotations would expand eventually. For now, everything was working.

The Clippers were playing at home, and they had title aspirations. They led at halftime by 4 points, but the Thunder took a 3-point lead at the beginning of the 4th quarter. OKC then turned it on, going on a 12-to-2 run to push their lead to 13 points and killing off the game. The Clippers were held to 1-of-8 shooting during that run with 2 balls stolen and a turnover. The Thunder ended up limiting the Clippers to just 14 points in the 4th quarter. Our old friend James Harden was Dorted into a 4-of-13 shooting night for just 12 points.

Nov 4th in OKC. Win vs Orlando 102-86.

This was an easy home win over the Magic. OKC scored 39 points in the first quarter, and they were up by 15 at halftime. The Thunder lead expanded to 26 at the end of the 3rd quarter as Isaiah Joe hit three straight 3-pointers. Orlando was held to 5-of-34 shooting on 3's.

The Thunder Offense

The 2025 Thunder offense was predicated on the idea that all five players on the floor can drive and can shoot. They also kept the ball moving. When a player caught a pass, he shot the ball if he was open. If he didn't have an open shot, he dribble-penetrated. If the drive didn't work, he immediately passed the ball on to the next player. The process then repeated- shoot, or penetrate. If the drive worked, he took it to the rim. If defensive help came, he passed out for an open player to take an uncontested shot.

All 12 Thunder players were really good 3-point shooters, except for Hartenstein (Caruso was the worst of the bunch, and he made a totally acceptable 35%). And all the players were good at dribbling past scrambling, off-balance defenders as the ball circulated around. All it took was one help defender moving over, and the dominoes started falling into place for open shots. And if the offense got stood up on a play, they just got the ball to Gil Goose. He could create a good shot in almost any scenario.

Another important piece of the Thunder's offensive philosophy was protecting the ball. The players did not give up turnovers, and they got back on defense when shots went up. The Thunder ended up with the NBA's best assist-to-turnover ratio, and also the fewest fast breaks allowed in the league. Their awesome defense forced the most steals in the league. The Thunder were so difficult to beat just by deploying their strategy of protecting the basketball while scoring easy baskets after turnovers.

Nov 6th in Denver. Loss vs Nuggets 122-124.

OKC must have embarrassed Denver on opening night, because the Nuggets came to play despite missing both Aaron Gordon and Jamal Murray. Michael Porter scored 24 points, with 21 of them coming in the 2nd half. And Nikola Jokic reminded the world who the best basketball player was in his matchup against SGA. He threw down a monster triple-double of 23 points, 20 rebounds, and 16 assists. Hartenstein could not return soon enough.

The game was really good. The Thunder were up 11 points at halftime, and they pushed their lead to 16 after the break. Midway through the 3rd, the Nuggets went on a 12-0 run fueled by Julian Strawther, and the teams ended the quarter tied. The game remained very close, and the Thunder had the lead at 108-106 with 5:26 to play when Denver went on a 17-7 run. The Thunder fought back to get the score within 2 points, and OKC fouled Peyton Watson with 16 seconds left. Watson missed both his free throws, giving OKC a chance to tie. Gil Goose drew Russ as his defender. He blew right by Russ on the left side for a layup, but Goose was met at the rim by Peyton Watson. Watson served Goose with a massive block at the buzzer to preserve the Denver victory.

Westbrook had a great game for the shorthanded Nuggets, scoring 29 points on 10-of-15 shooting. J-Dub almost had a triple double with 29 points, 10 rebounds, and 9 assists for the Thunder. The Thunder had 15 steals, with Lu Dort contributing 3 steals and 2 blocks, and Alex Caruso adding 4 steals and 2 blocks himself.

Nov 8th in OKC. Win vs Houston 126-107.

This was the first game of the season that I attended in person, and it was my four-year-old son's first Thunder game ever. It wasn't much of a contest, though, as the Thunder raced out to a 24-point lead while scoring 75 first-half points. Gil Goose started the game 10-of-11, and he ended up with 29 points.

I got to see up close how much the Thunder players loved each other. Their camaraderie was obvious on television, but during pregame warmups they just had a joy about them. It was a stark contrast to the Houston Rockets, who seemed very frustrated before the game even started. They had started the season poorly, despite being very talented. During the game, Ime Udoka, Fred Van

Vleet, and Dillon Brooks all confronted Jalen Green for his lackadaisical defense, and for jacking up bad shots. After one missed defensive assignment led to an easy Thunder basket, Dillon Brooks followed Green back to the bench, yelling in his ear the whole way.

Jalen Green finished the game 5-of-14. After witnessing this Houston team's problems in person, I was not surprised when they lost in the first round of the playoffs to the 7-seed. Nor was I surprised when they traded the former number 2 pick Jalen Green away in the summer.

Nov 10th in OKC. Loss vs Warriors 116-127.

This was one of the worst games of the season for OKC, as the old men of the Warriors tried to prove they were still relevant by beating the Thunder. Golden State was up by 7 points at halftime, and then had a monster 3rd quarter, taking a 30-point lead while outscoring the Thunder 21-42. The Thunder did bring the game back within 6 points with 4:46 to play, but they couldn't get any closer. Golden State was the first team all season to shoot over 50% against the Thunder defense.

The big news from the game happened in the 6th minute, when Andrew Wiggins drove baseline for a dunk. Chet rose up to block his shot, and their bodies collided and entangled. Our baby giraffe Chet fell very awkwardly and landed horizontally, hard. He had to be helped to the locker room, and was diagnosed with a broken hip. He would be out indefinitely.

Was the season over already? Holmgren was off to a great start, and so was the team. But all four big men on the roster were now out hurt (Frankenstein, J-Will, Kenrich, and Chet). And true to Thunder protocol, these injuries were not updated. Instead, the situations were treated as closely guarded state secrets. I didn't even know what Kenrich's injury was at this point (he had knee surgery just before preseason). Did this mean that Ousmane Dieng was about to get a huge run of games? How could OKC survive that? I jokingly texted my friends that it was time to bring back Bismack Biyombo.

10 Game Summary

Overall, the first ten OKC games had been a huge success. The Thunder won 8 of the 10 games, and the closest winning margin was when the Spurs lost by a massive 12 points. And 7 of these opponents would end up making the playoffs. This Thunder team was killing their opponents, and the OKC defense was suffocating. Oklahoma City's only losses were a very close game to the Nuggets (see you in the postseason), and the loss against the Warriors after our young players had to witness Golden State murder Chet in front of them.

Nov 11th in OKC. Win vs Clippers 134-128.

With all of his big men hurt, Coach Daigneault's solution at center was Jalen Williams, our 6-foot 6-inch small forward. The Thunder would embrace their size disadvantage, and they would swarm the low post when needed. And who would the opposition's center, like Zubac in this game, guard at the other end? Zubac surely couldn't guard J-Dub attacking on the dribble from the 3-point line.

Kenrich Williams returned from injury for his first game of the season. He could play as an undersized center as well, but he only got 5 minutes in this game. Aaron Wiggins moved into the starting lineup, joined by Isaiah Joe. Cason and Caruso came off the bench. James Harden had 17 points, 11 rebounds and 9 assists, but he was Dorted into 5-of-15 shooting. Although the small Thunder lineup was outrebounded 47-to-29, they scored 32 points off the 24 turnovers they forced.

OKC was up on LA by 13 points at the half, and they pushed the lead to 20 points with 6:16 left in the 3rd. The Clippers came back with a 14-5 run to make it 92-81 with 2:51 left, and kept tightening the game from there. The Clippers were down by 5 points with 42 seconds left, 130-125, when Zubac got the ball in the low post, and spun by J-Dub to dunk while being fouled. He made his free throw to make it a 2-point game. Gil Goose then ran down the clock to 23 seconds, and spun into a step-back jumper on the left corner of the box. He missed, but he was fouled by Derrick Jones on the shot. Goose made both free throws to put the lead to 4 points. Harden then tried to create at the 3-point line with time running out, but Lu Dort stood him up, causing him to slip and then tying up the ball. OKC won the jump ball, and LA wasn't able to foul before J-Dub was released down the court for an uncontested breakaway dunk to finish the game off.

SGA finished with a career-high 45 points. He also had 9 assists and 5 steals. He had started his MVP season in dominant fashion.

Nov 13th in OKC. Win vs Pelicans 106-88.

The Pelicans pretended to have title hopes in the offseason. Those hopes were already up in smoke this early in the season, as they had just 3 wins and 8 losses. New Orleans was missing Zion Williamson, CJ McCollum, Herb Jones, and Dejounte Murray, so Brandon Boston started and played 31 minutes.

OKC used a nine-man rotation. Cason Wallace and Isaiah Joe started with Goose, J-Dub, and Dort. Wiggins came off the bench with Kenrich, Ajay, and Dieng. Caruso sat out. The Thunder's small lineup got outrebounded again, 58-to-31. But they made up for it by forcing 24 turnovers with 16 steals. The Thunder closed the 1st quarter with a 24-8 run, and led by 4 points at the half. With the game tied at 59 in the 3rd quarter, the Thunder surged ahead with a 16-0 run. The Pelicans had conceded 4 steals and 2 blocks while shooting 0-for-5. The Thunder led by 14 at the end of the 3rd, and the game was over. Cason Wallace had 5 steals, and J-Dub produced a monster stat line of 31 points, 6 rebounds, 7 assists, and 4 steals.

Nov 15th in OKC. Win vs Phoenix 99-83.

This game was also OKC's first NBA Cup group-stage game, but Phoenix forgot to show up. Kevin Durant and Brad Beal didn't play (the Phoenix injury report should have said OUT: Too Scared). OKC, despite missing their big men and using J-Dub at center, outrebounded Phoenix and blocked 11 of their shots. OKC flew out to a 29-14 lead in the 1st quarter. The Thunder then led by 25 points in the second half. Devin Booker, the Suns' only "star" who played, was Dorted into 12 points on 2-of-10 shooting. Phoenix sucks.

Nov 17th in OKC. Loss to Dallas 119-121.

The Mavericks were missing their fat superstar Luka Doncic, but OKC still lost. It was so frustrating to continually struggle against Dallas, especially while watching PJ Washington play like an All-Star. The Thunder didn't have Caruso for this game, and they also were still missing their three bigs. Those absences forced OKC to play a nine-man rotation that included rookie Dillon Jones. Dallas killed Oklahoma City on the boards, 53-29.

Despite the loss, it was an exciting game with a great finish. Dallas was winning big, 109-119, with just 1:30 left when the Thunder went on a furious 10-2 run. The run started with a Kenrich layup, a Kenrich steal, and then a J-Dub steal that created another layup for Kenrich. A forced turnover on Dallas turned into a J-Dub layup, and then a Goose 3-pointer pulled the score within 3 points with 25 seconds left.

Kyrie Irving took the inbounds pass in the frontcourt. He got into the lane before picking up his dribble, expecting a foul with so little time remaining. No foul came. Goose eventually tied him up for a jump ball with 8 seconds left, 118-121. Goose won the jump ball, and Dallas tipped the ball out of bounds for an OKC possession. Ajay, who was playing in these crunch time minutes, inbounded to Goose, and he was immediately fouled. 4 seconds remained. Goose made his first free throw, 119-121, then purposely missed the 2nd. A melee ensued, and the rebound bounced around to Lu Dort, who gathered and turned to launch a contested 3-pointer at the buzzer for the win, but he missed.

PJ freaking Washington had 27 points and 17 rebounds. Jeff texted us, "if I never have to watch Dillon Jones play again, I'll be okay. He sucks." The poor rookie had already lost him just 14 games into the season.

Nov 19th in San Antonio. Loss vs Spurs 104-110.

The Thunder lost their 2nd game in a row, and this one was to the lowly San Antonio Spurs, a .500 team playing without Victor Wembanyama. To make matters worse, this was an NBA Cup group-stage game. J-Dub was still playing center, and he finished with 27 points, 10 rebounds, and 5 steals. But the Spurs had 7 players in double-figures.

San Antonio had a 25-3 run starting in the 2nd quarter, and they led by 16 points at the end of the 3rd. The Thunder tried to come back with a 27-12 run to end the game, but they couldn't get it done. OKC was killed by their 3-point shooting. Dort and J-Dub shot a combined 2-of-14, while Adam Flagler, a Thunder player that I hope I don't ever have to mention again, was 1-of-7 from 3 in just 10 minutes of play.

Nov 20th in OKC. Win vs Portland 109-99.

The Jalen Williams experiment at center did not go great. The Thunder won 3 and lost 2, and were hugely outrebounded in 3 of those games. But the experiment was over, because Isaiah Hartenstein was back to make his Thunder debut. And it was a great debut too, as he had 13 points, 14 rebounds, and 4 blocks in 29 minutes. I was immediately sold.

I texted to my friends, "Frankenstein's way, way better than I expected. That guy is seriously good at basketball."

Portland played Oklahoma City close until the end, and the Blazers had six players in double-figures. But they committed 24 turnovers, including 14 steals, and suffered 8 blocked shots.

The Thunder Defense

The accountability and standard of play on this Thunder team was something to behold. The players were well aware that Coach Daigneault was not afraid to adjust their play time up or down depending on their performance and effort. The individual players fought and sacrificed for each other and for their collective goals. The team had a culture like that of military squadrons. Individual needs and desires came second to the team's success. It was no coincidence that the players regularly referred to each other as "brothers" and "family".

The result of this culture that Coach Daigneault had implemented, unique in the NBA, was an intensity on defense that would break the league. A typical Thunder defensive play had non-stop, suffocating pressure on the ball. Usually, Lu Dort picked up the player bringing the ball up the court, but Cason Wallace and Alex Caruso often got that assignment as well. They did not wait for their opponent to advance into a play before they began engaging him. They pressed close to their opponents, swiping and probing, trying to steal the ball, as soon as it was advanced into the frontcourt. There was limited switching on defense this season, and the team almost always fought over screens instead of sitting underneath them.

Behind that first line of defense from the guards were Gil Goose and J-Dub, two players with freakishly long arms for their height. They excelled at poking the ball away from dribblers when least expected, and at deflecting the ball in passing lanes.

If a player snuck through those first two lines of defensive resistance, coming to the rim to meet him was Chet Holmgren. He was one of the NBA's best shot-blockers and help defenders.

Most teams reserved full defensive intensity for the end of a game. Some teams had one or two "defensive specialists" that gave their maximum effort, while their other teammates stood around, watching. It was such a contrast to watch all of the Thunder play with relentless intensity, game after game, play after play.

This was the culture that Presti and Daigneault wanted, and it took a long time to build. Since the tank season of 2021, almost every postgame interview sounded the same. Players kept saying things like, "Just trying to play hard on defense" or "Just trying to get better at defense," no matter what the question was.

Years of emphasis and buy-in resulted in one of the greatest defenses in league history. This, in turn, resulted in one of the greatest teams in league history. If I had to sum up the 2025 Thunder season in a sentence, it was "Fast breaks off of steals all day long."

Here are some relevant OKC defensive statistics for the 2025 season:

107.5 Defensive Rating-	1st
10.3 Steals per Game-	1st
5.7 Blocks per Game-	2nd
17.0 Turnovers Forced per Game-	1st
21 Deflections per game-	1st
22.7 Points off of Turnovers per Game-	1st
.436 Opponent's Field Goal %-	1st
.513 Opponent's Effective Field Goal %-	1st
106.5 Points Allowed per 100 Possessions-	1st

The incredible defense described above created bountiful fast break opportunities and easy points. This sparked scoring runs that often turned tight games into blowouts. That defense, combined with the Thunder offense that led the league in turnover percentage (meaning they didn't give away fast break opportunities), set the stage for the team's success.

Now that I've described the Thunder's excellent team defense, I'll rate the players individually. Beforehand, I need to mention that although Jaylin Williams did not make this list, he had been particularly brilliant at drawing charges over the past three years.

The Thunder's Best Defensive Players

Isaiah Hartenstein. I considered Frankenstein to be a very good defender, but I didn't have him on this list until I saw he had the best Defensive Rating in the entire league, and by a large margin (Defensive Rating measures how many points a player gives up per 100 possessions. The top 4 players were all from the Thunder; #5 was Wembanyama). Isaiah also had the 16th best block percentage in the entire league. Hartenstein was only the Thunder's 7th best defender.

Chet Holmgren. He was an absolutely top-notch help defender and premier rim protector. Chet averaged 2.2 blocks per game, which would have been 3rd best in the NBA behind Wemby and Walker Kessler. His average of 2.9 blocks per 36 minutes also would have been 3rd best in the NBA. I did not think his one-on-one post defending or his defensive rebounding had been very good, though. Holmgren was only the Thunder's 6th best defender.

Shai Gilgeous-Alexander. SGA was an above-average one-on-one defender, very tough to get around or above, and he was capable of using his long arms to poke at the ball around the opponent's back while keeping his body in front of the player. Goose was 2nd in the NBA in steals, and he had the NBA's 3rd best Defensive Rating. Goose received votes for the NBA's Defensive Player of the Year in each of the last two seasons. Gil Goose was only the Thunder's 5th best defender.

Jalen Williams. J-Dub finished 2nd in Defensive Rating while guarding every position from center to point guard. He was 7th in the NBA in steals per game with 1.6. His quickness and length made him a great one-on-one defender. He was deservedly voted onto the NBA All-Defense 2nd team. Jalen Williams was only the Thunder's 4th best defender.

Cason Wallace. Cason was only 20 years-old during the 2025 season, and just in his 2nd year. He broke into the lineup as a rookie due to his outstanding defense. He was neither really tall nor really big, but he was very fast, very quick, and very tough. His quick hands and anticipation caused havoc for opponents, and Cason was 3rd in the league in steals per game and 4th in steals per 36 minutes. He also finished 4th in Defensive Rating. Cason Wallace was only the Thunder's 3rd best defender.

Lu Dort. Lu was a steel cannonball with human skin stretched over the top. An Oklahoma living legend, he has been guarding the opposing team's best player for six straight years now. He was regularly cited in player surveys as one of the toughest defenders in the league. Dort's legs were so strong that he's almost impossible to pick, as most centers usually got knocked off-balance by contact from Dort, not the other way around. Lu finally made his first, long-overdue All-NBA Defensive 1st Team this season. Any talk of the Thunder defense has started with Lu Dort for years. And Lu Dort was only the Thunder's 2nd best defender.

Alex Caruso. AC was used sparingly this season, playing only 54 games and averaging just 19 minutes a game. But when he played, the Thunder defense went up to another level. He did not play enough to qualify for All Defensive Team honors in 2025, but he was no doubt worthy of it. He was so pesky guarding point guards. When off the ball, it's as if he was seeing 3 seconds into the future, jumping passes and double-teaming opponents at the perfect time. He directed the team's defense. Caruso was big enough to mix it up against forwards. And in the playoffs, Caruso was the player who finally contained Nikola Jokic's offense, despite being half his size and a full head shorter. In a team full of great, great defenders, Alex Caruso was the best of the bunch.

Nov 25th in Sacramento. Win vs Kings 130-109.

The Thunder led a close game at halftime by 1 point. It was 79-78 with 4:36 remaining in the 3rd when the Thunder went on a 13-2 run to take control. OKC shot 5-of-6 from the field, while the Kings missed 4 straight 3-point shots and Sabonis committed 2 charges. That run made the score 92-80 with 1:37 left, and the Thunder closed the game out from there.

A healthy Hartenstein had joined a new starting lineup that also included Goose, J-Dub, Dort, and Wiggins, with Joe, Ajay, Cason, and Kenrich coming off the bench. Caruso sat the game out. Gil Goose had 37 points. DeAaron Fox received the Dorture Chamber treatment, scoring just 14 points on 5-of-15 shooting. Brad pointed out that DeAaron Fox was in the top 6 of the NBA's scoring chart, but OKC shut him down. I texted to my friends, "Thunder defense so awesome."

Nov 27th in SF. Win vs Warriors 105-101.

The second game of this four-game road trip presented the team with a chance to avenge one of its only losses of the season. Caruso, Chet, and J-Will were still unavailable, so Ajay, Kenrich, and Dillon Jones all got 12-16 minutes of play time. Steph Curry was injured for the Warriors, and former Thunder player Lindy Waters started in his place.

The Thunder had a big 1st quarter with 39 points. The Warriors, having broken Chet Holmgren the last time they played, tried the same with Jalen Williams. With six minutes left in the first half, they injured his eye, forcing him out of the game. The Thunder was up by 12 points at the half, but their lead was down to 1 at the end of the 3rd quarter of this tight game.

OKC was still ahead, 97-96, with 3:51 to go. Both teams combined to miss the next nine shots, and Goose finally hit a step back 3 to go up by 4 points with 1:25 left. Draymond missed a 3 on the next possession, but Lu Dort was called for a charge with 49 seconds to go. Jonathon Kuminga then attempted a jumper for Golden State, but he missed, and Hartenstein was fouled with 26 seconds left. Hartenstein missed his second free throw, and Draymond Green received a quick pass in the lane for a wide-open dunk. Golden State's deficit was cut to 3 points, but only 19 seconds remained. Hartenstein was fouled again, and he missed another free throw. GSW quickly ran a couple of picks for Andrew Wiggins, and he attempted a 3 that was contested by Dort. The 3-point shot went in, and it was a 1-point game with 11 seconds left. Gil Goose was fouled after the inbounds pass, and the Thunder again went 1-of-2 from the free throw line. 7 seconds to go. Two-point lead. Golden State was barely able to inbound the ball to Draymond, who was blanketed in the corner. Andrew Wiggins peeled away from him, and Draymond lofted a perfect pass over the defense for an alley-oop layup to tie the game. But Lu Dort recovered just in time to deflect Wiggins' shot and preserve the victory.

Nov 29th in LA. Win vs the Lakers 101-93.

This was the Thunder's 3rd NBA Cup group-stage game, and it was a must-win game for the Lakers if they wanted to defend their NBA Cup title from 2023. It was a close game, and OKC led by 1 point before Gil Goose hit a 3-point shot with 1:35 left. LeBron followed with a missed 3-point attempt, but Gil Goose also missed a 3 on his next possession. Max Christie then made a layup, cutting the score to two points. Gil Goose sealed the game with two free throws.

Dec 1st in Houston. Loss vs Rockets 116-119.

The Rockets were playing great basketball, with 12 wins in their last 15 games. This game was close throughout, with 16 different ties, but the Rockets outscored the Thunder 20-28 in the 4th quarter to win. Gil Goose missed a 3 with 1:15 left, but Hartenstein fought to secure the offensive rebound. He passed the ball out to Cason Wallace, who hit a 3-pointer to tie.

Fred Van Vleet missed a 3 for Houston on their next possession, but the ball was tied up in the fight for the rebound, and Houston won the jump ball.

Sengun tried to dribble into a post-up on Hartenstein, but he slipped and fell onto his butt. As the Thunder swarmed down on him, Sengun was somehow able to make a pass from the ground to a cutting Dillon Brooks. Brooks hit a running jumper as the shot clock expired, putting Houston up by 2 points with 33 seconds left. Gil Goose then missed a jump shot with the game on the line. Van Vleet was fouled, and he made his free throws with 4 seconds left. J-Dub hit a quick 3-pointer, but it was too late to save the game.

Alex Caruso had missed his 4th straight game. Fred Van Vleet had a monster game of 5 3-pointers and 38 points for Houston. Probably just as significant to the Rockets' win was Jalen Green only took 6 shots.

20 Game Summary

The Thunder now had 15 wins and 5 losses in the first 20 games of the season. Coach Daigneault was still figuring out his player rotations. With Jaylin Williams and Chet Holmgren injured, plus Alex Caruso missing games, Cason Wallace, Dillon Jones, Ajay Mitchell, and Ousmane Dieng got opportunities to play. Aaron Wiggins and Isaiah Joe were occasionally starting games. And Isaiah Hartenstein had been beyond great. It had been a very positive start to the season.

Cason Wallace

Cason Wallace was coming into his own in the 2025 season. He had played one college season at Kentucky before being drafted by the Thunder with the 10th pick. Sam Presti liked Cason so much that he traded up to pick him, giving up some of OKC's cap space (to absorb the Davis Bertans' contract) in the process.

Wallace joined a good Oklahoma City team in 2024, and he made it better. He played over 20 minutes per game as a rookie, and he even started 13 times. Cason shot a very good 42% from 3 and played excellent defense, but on offense that season he was very deferential to his teammates. He rarely drove into the lane or initiated any offense himself.

In his second season, Cason made over 35% of his 3's while averaging 28 minutes per game and starting 43 times. His defense was spectacular. He will be in the discussion for All-Defense teams if he can win more minutes on the court. Importantly, Cason was way more assertive on offense in the 2nd half of the 2025 season than he was in his first year-and-a-half on the team. He increased his scoring average to 11 points per game in his final 21 games after averaging just 7 points per game before that. Wallace had the tools to be an offensive power. He was good at using his quickness to drive to the basket, and was extremely fast down the court after turnovers. And Cason was explosive on dunks.

I hope Cason develops a confidence similar to what Aaron Wiggins had acquired, where he was always looking to create as a primary weapon. I think he's good enough to do it. Either way, Cason Wallace has had a great first two years to start his career.

Not that you'd hear him talk about it. In two years of watching him I had rarely heard him speak or even show any emotion at all. Wallace just did the job in front of him. His silence was probably another thing Presti loved about him.

Dec 3rd in OKC. Win vs Utah Jazz 133-106.

This was the Thunder's last NBA Cup group-stage game. If they won, they would advance to the playoff rounds. No problem. The Jazz sucked. The Thunder were up by 12 points at halftime, and extended their lead to 27 by the end of the 3rd, helped by 18 steals and 29 turnovers. The Jazz dropped to 4 wins and 17 losses.

Dec 5th in Toronto. Win vs Raptors 129-92.

This was one of OKC's easiest wins of the season. Toronto started out shooting 5-of-25, and the Thunder were up by 17 points in the 1st quarter. OKC had 9 steals and 9 blocks in the first half, and their lead at halftime had grown to 25 points. OKC finished with 15 steals and 20 forced turnovers, and the bench mob of Kenrich, Caruso, Wiggins, Cason, and Ajay were responsible for 10 of those steals.

Isaiah Joe

The Thunder had suffered for years and years from terrible 3-point shooting. Andre Roberson spent four years in OKC's starting lineup, and during all four years he lived completely unguarded in the corner. No opponent would even take a step in his direction when he got the ball. Instead, they'd turn their backs to him to find someone to box out. Roberson would often pass the ball away, but if he launched a shot, it was anybody's guess where it would land. If you told me right now that his career 3-point percentage was 6%, I would believe it. On his podcast this year, Stephen Jackson said to Kevin Durant, "(Roberson) couldn't hit a house if he was in the kitchen."

Roberson was the worst shooter that OKC had deployed, but he wasn't alone. It's hard to name any good 3-point shooters from the first 12 years of the Thunder's existence. Kevin Durant, of course, and Kevin Martin for one year, and... anybody else?

The NBA had changed in the 2010's into a 3-point shooting league, and thankfully Presti had started to acquire good shooters. In 2022, Presti signed Isaiah Joe, a lanky 6'5" guard and 3-point specialist. Joe was the Gatorade Player of the Year for Arkansas in high school in 2018 (his teammate was Thunder player Jaylin Williams). He then played for two years in college at Arkansas before getting drafted by the 76ers with the 49th pick. Joe was used sparingly over two seasons in Philadelphia, having played in just 96 games. They released him just before the 2022 season. Philadelphia had Tyrese Maxey and James Harden as starters in 2022, with DeAnthony Melton and Tulsa's own Shake Milton backing them up. They also had just drafted Jaden Springer, so Isaiah Joe was squeezed out.

Joe had shot 35% from 3 for Philly, which wasn't bad, but wasn't great either. However, Presti saw something that he liked, and quickly signed him to a 3-year/ $6 million contract. OKC was handsomely rewarded for Presti's intra-league scouting. Joe has averaged over 41% on 3-pointers for the Thunder on a high volume of shots, and he had been a very important part of the Thunder's success the past three years. Joe was rewarded for his play, too. In the summer of 2024, he re-signed for 4-years/ $48 million, a very reasonable salary for a wing player with his shooting capabilities.

Joe was the rare player who, if he set up for an uncontested shot, it was a shock if it didn't go in. He must be defended at the 3-point line, and that stretched the defense in a way that most Thunder teams weren't ever able to.

During the 2025 season Joe started 16 games while shooting 41% from 3. He hit at least 3 3-pointers in 33 games, and scored in double-digits in 35 of his 74 games. In a game against Utah, he made 10 3-pointers. It was so great to finally have a player who always made his deep shots, after years spent watching opposing players do it to us.

Dec 7th in NOLA. Win vs Pelicans 119-109.

This was an unusual game. Brandon Ingram only played 19 minutes before suffering an ankle injury that would keep him out for most of the rest of the season. And Zion Williamson also wasn't playing. The Thunder were up by 12 points at the end of the 1st quarter, and blowing the Pelicans out by 26 points at halftime. Despite those setbacks, the Pelicans fought back, holding the Thunder to just 42 points in the 2nd half. New Orleans brought the lead down to 9 points with 3:31 left before the Thunder scored five straight to seal the victory.

I texted to my friends, "Thunder are so damn good on defense. They looked lost on those Gil Goose double-teams in the 4th quarter. But God are they good on defense." New Orleans was not good at defense. They dropped to 5 and 19, and their team sucked.

Dec 10th in OKC. Win vs Dallas 118-104.

OKC scored a huge win in the quarterfinals of the NBA Cup, and it was against a Dallas team that usually had the Thunder's number. PJ Washington the God didn't play, and Doncic the Fat was held to just 5-of-15 shooting for 16 points with 11 rebounds and 5 assists in 40 minutes. The Thunder only had a 3-point lead at halftime, but they started the 2nd half with a 13 – 2 run to stretch their lead to 14. The game was never in doubt after that. All five Thunder starters scored in double-figures, and OKC out-rebounded Dallas on the offensive glass 17 to 7. OKC also scored 36 points off 19 Dallas turnovers.

Oklahoma City was headed to Vegas, baby!

Dec 14th in Vegas. Win vs Rockets 111-96.

Oklahoma City had made it to the semifinal of the NBA Cup! Both defenses clamped down in the 1st half. Houston was up 18-20 at the end of the 1st, and winning 41-42 at halftime. Houston played just a 7-man rotation, and 6 of their players scored in double-figures, while the Rockets outrebounded OKC 19-to-4 on the offensive end. However, the Rockets only shot 24% from 3, and just 37% overall.

The Thunder were up by 5 points with 8 minutes left before going on a 13-3 run to lead 97-82 with 5 minutes to go. OKC shot 4-for-7 during their run, while the Rockets shot 1-of-5 with 2 turnovers. After single-handedly giving the Thunder one of their few losses of the season in the previous Rockets game, Fred Van Vleet went just 1-of-11 on 3-pointers in this one. The Rockets might not have been done with Vegas, but Vegas was done with them.

Dec 17th in Las Vegas. Loss vs Bucks 81-97.

It was a crushing loss for the Thunder with a trophy on the line in the NBA Cup Final. Seemingly nothing went right. The Thunder's previous low score this season had been 99 points, so 81 points was an especially abysmal performance. And OKC had 50 points at halftime!

With 3 minutes left in the 3rd quarter, it was a 5-point game. But Milwaukee went on a 19-5 run to lead by 19 points in the 4th quarter, putting the game out of reach. The Thunder's record was now 20-and-1 when leading after 3 quarters, but 0-and-5 when tied or trailing.

Cason and Hartenstein shot well at a combined 8-for-13, but the rest of the Thunder shot a horrific 29% on their field goal attempts. OKC also made just 16% of their 3-pointers (5-for-32). Gil Goose went 8-of-24 for only 21 points. Johnny Boy didn't forget to show up for Milwaukee with a title on the line, as he had a monster game of 26 points, 19 rebounds, and 10 assists. The Bucks were playing their best basketball of the season. They were now 13- 3 in their previous 16 games.

The Thunder were a great team, but were they good enough to win when it mattered? These Bucks players had climbed that mountain before, and this comprehensive win left doubts about OKC. The Thunder had delivered their worst performance of the entire regular season in one of their most important games of the year. Could OKC learn from what went wrong, and ascend to another level?

Dec 19th in Orlando. Win vs Magic 105-99.

The Thunder bounced back from the disappointment in Vegas with a tough win in Orlando. The Magic didn't have their two best players, Paulo Banchero and Franz Wagner, and they had lost 3 of their last 4 games. The Thunder had an 18-4 run to start the 2nd quarter, which gave them a 19-point lead at halftime. However, the Magic pushed back in the 2nd half, cutting the lead to 86-83 with 9:42 left in the game. J-Dub then kickstarted a 14-to-3 run with two lay-ups and a dunk over three consecutive possessions to put the game away.

The Thunder recorded 15 steals in the game. Steals were the key to OKC's core identity (OKC led the NBA in steals in both 2024 and 2025). The Thunder's ball pressure was high every game. Even when they didn't get steals, their pressure caused shot clock violations, deflections, and bad shots. In general, this pressure put the other team out of their offensive rhythms. All this chaos also generated easy fast-break points for OKC, and resulted in many big 3rd quarter runs that directly led to Thunder wins.

Most other NBA teams did not play like this. And no NBA team was better at sustaining intense defensive pressure than the Thunder. OKC would score 10 unanswered points 109 times in the regular season and playoffs. The next best team did it 82 times.

Dec 20th in Miami. Win vs Heat 104-97.

Miami fought hard in this close game, despite Jimmy Butler only playing 7 minutes due to illness. Miami was up by 3 points in the 3rd quarter, but OKC went on a 10-0 run to take control. Miami kept the lead to single-digits for most of the 4th quarter, but every time they tried to inch closer than 5 points, the Thunder would answer back. J-Dub finished with 33 points for OKC, and Gil Goose scored 25 points, which was his 17th game in a row with at least 25.

Jalen Williams

Here's an interesting question that's occasionally been asked- Was Jalen Williams better than Gil Goose was? It's actually difficult to come to a conclusion after 3 years. That's how good of a player J-Dub had been.

Jalen Williams was an amazing basketball talent. He could shoot 3's (over 38% for his career), was an explosive dunker, and had become a really good dribble-penetrator. J-Dub's ball-handling skills had greatly improved. He was 6'6", and could finish at the rim with either hand.

But was he a better player than Goose? SGA had taken over the Thunder by his 3rd season, and averaged almost 24 points and 6 assists per game. But OKC was terrible that year, and Goose only played 35 games before he was shut down with "injury" so that the Thunder could tank. Goose finally made an All-Star team and the All-NBA team in his 5th season.

In his 3rd season in 2025, J-Dub averaged 21 points and 5 assists per game, and played outstanding defense. He made his 1st All-Star team and All-NBA team, and he also got an All-Defense team honor.

Jalen Williams' trajectory had been steadily upwards, scoring and assisting more and taking more shots every year...

	1st Year	2nd Year	3rd Year
PPG	14	19	21
APG	3.3	4.5	5.1
3-pt Atts	2.7	3.4	4.9
FGA	10.6	14	16.9

In fact, that chart looks very similar to Gil Goose's rise…

	1st Year	2nd Year	3rd Year
PPG	11	19	23.7
APG	3.3	3.3	5.9
3-pt Atts	1.7	3.6	4.9
FGA	8.7	14.5	16.1

My answer was that Goose was better than J-Dub. Goose was clearly the driving force of the Thunder, and he was the NBA's MVP. But I will say that J-Dub was developing on Goose's same trajectory, and there was a good chance J-Dub will end up being a player of similar caliber (and the Thunder got both of them in the Paul George trade).

What the Thunder had was Jordan and Pippen lite. That was how high the ceiling reached for this duo. I grew up on Micheal Jordan, and I'm not arguing that Goose was better than MJ. Jordan was the best basketball player of all time.

The comparison certainly worked physically. Goose was a 6'6" shooting guard who always was at the top of the scoring charts by driving to the rim and getting to the line. He was joined by his small forward, a defensive specialist who provided ball-handling and secondary offense, and was a great player in his own right.

I absolutely will compare J-Dub to Pippen. They both had great control, excellent balance, basketball smarts, and toughness. They both guarded all five positions, and were stronger than their size would indicate. They were the rare players who could shut down quick point guards on the perimeter, and also bang with big centers in the post.

J-Dub after just 3 years was not as good as Pippen defensively. Pippen was one of the NBA's greatest defenders in an era of great defenses. But offensively, J-Dub was already almost his equal. Pippen's scoring statistics were hamstrung, because Micheal Jordan took most of their shots. But in 1994 and 1995, when Jordan was "retired", it was famously Pippen's time to shine as the Bull's 1st option on offense. He had the best offensive output of his career at 22 points and 5.6 assists per game in 1994, and then 21 points and 5.2 assists per game in 1995. Pippen was 1st team All-NBA both seasons. J-Dub was already in that neighborhood offensively.

Everyone knew Jalen Williams was a great talent. But I was comparing him to Gil Goose and Scottie Pippen? For many people, these pages about J-Dub might be the most ludicrous assertions I will make in the entire book. But J-Dub had a good chance to become as great as those two players. Jordan and Pippen, 2.0? That's what I can't stop thinking about. And the 6 championships that they won.

Dec 23rd in OKC. Win vs Wizards 123-105.

The Wizards were a horrible team as usual, as they had started the season with 4 wins and 22 losses. But in this game they made 16 of their first 32 3's. They also scored 63 points in the first half, one of the highest totals against the Thunder all season. Still, they trailed by 4 points.

The Thunder went on a 19-to-2 run in the 4th quarter to pull away completely. The Wizards went 0-for-5 during that run, and had the ball stolen twice and a shot blocked. The Thunder had 15 steals in the game, with the bench mob of Cason, Caruso, and Kenrich combining to swipe 7 of them. Meanwhile, the Wizards missed their last 11 attempts from beyond the arc.

Gil Goose had 41 points and 9 rebounds, and Ajay had 16 points and 12 rebounds in just 22 minutes. Isaiah Joe was in the starting lineup with Chet still out. Another positive from the game was the return of Jaylin Williams, who played 8 minutes. He had missed the first 27 games of the season with a hamstring injury.

The Thunder had 23 wins and just 5 losses, but they were somewhat flying under the radar. Over in the Eastern United States, the Cleveland Cavaliers began the season with 15 straight wins, and they had the best record in the league at 26 and 4. Were the Cavs better than even the Thunder?

Dec 26th in Indiana. Win vs Pacers 120-114.

In a preview of the NBA Finals, the Thunder came from behind to beat the Pacers on the road on Boxing Day. It was a very odd decision to omit Oklahoma City from a showcase game on Christmas Day. They had one of the league's star players, and the best record in the West in the 2024 season. I was pretty sure that December 25, 2024, would be the last work-free Christmas Day for Gil Goose and the rest of the team for a very long time.

The Pacers were winning by 15 points in the first quarter, and they were still up by 8 at halftime. The Thunder whittled Indiana's lead down to 1 point at the end of the 3rd quarter. The Pacers were still winning 103-107 with 3:31 left in the game, when the Thunder went on an 8-0 run to pull into the lead. Benedict Mathurin then made 2 free throws, cutting the lead to 2 points with 1:16 left. Goose followed with a 3-pointer. On the Pacers' next possession, Aaron Nembhard missed a 3. Gil Goose was then fouled, and he made his free throws to put OKC up 116-109, and Indiana couldn't come back. It was a close game, though, and a taste of what would come in the Finals. Gil Goose had an outstanding performance, shooting 15-of-22 for 45 points, 7 rebounds, and 8 assists, and Haliburton only had 4 points in 35 minutes.

Dec 28th in Charlotte. Win vs Hornets 106-94.

The team flew to North Carolina to scrimmage against this suckass, 7-win team, losers of 14 of their last 15 games. LaMelo Ball was missing, as usual, while the Thunder were without Chet, Dort, Cason, and Caruso. That left starting spots for Ajay and Wiggins, and both played over 30 minutes each. The game was never close, as the Thunder led by 15 points at halftime, and by 16 at the end of the 3rd quarter.

30 Game Summary

Oklahoma City now had 25 wins and 5 losses, and they were on a 10-game winning streak (The NBA Cup Final did not count as an official NBA game). The Thunder were rounding into shape and certainly were title contenders. However, their tough upcoming schedule would test their strength. Coach Daigneault still was alternating his 5th starter, while J-Dub was learning to be the team creator when Gil Goose was on the bench. Hartenstein had been a revelation with 12 double-doubles in his first 15 games.

Isaiah Hartenstein

The Thunder had been a really good team in 2024, but their rebounding had been horrible. They were bottom of the league in many measurements of rebounding proficiency. The team was glaringly missing a classic big man.

I was very skeptical that the backup center for the New York Knicks could solve the problem. My issue with Hartenstein was that every player on the Thunder was capable of shooting 3's, and that opened space for Gil Goose to drive to the basket. How would Hartenstein fit into that framework? He couldn't shoot 3's, so his defender could lay off of him to help clog the lane. The Thunder also was collectively very fast. I imagined Frankenstein as a plodding 7-footer who would be unable to keep up.

It was immediately obvious that my concerns were unwarranted. Hartenstein fit perfectly into the team. He was quick for a big guy, and very good at setting picks. He excelled at initiating the offense, as he knew when and where to drop passes on the pick-and-roll. He also was competent at throwing lobs, and brilliant at bounce passes to his teammates on backdoor cuts. As a roller, Hartenstein was a tough box out, and he won many offensive rebounds. His signature shot was a short-range, left-handed push shot within the box that he put up so quickly it was rarely, if ever, blocked. It felt like he made 96% of those shots during the regular season.

Opposing defenses couldn't find an advantage with Hartenstein on the floor because his decision making was so good. He could go in any direction with the ball despite not being a deep shooting threat himself (He did attempt 19 3-pointers in 2025. He missed all 19. It was hilarious).

Hartenstein's 10.7 rebounds per game would have been the 8th best in the league if he had played enough. He averaged 13.8 rebounds per 36 minutes, which was the 10th best rate in the NBA. The Thunder's team rebounding numbers shot way up with Hartenstein in 2025, after finishing at the bottom of the league the previous year. He was excellent defensively, too, and he always played hard.

Hartenstein came out of nowhere. He was a 2nd round pick by Houston in 2017, and they barely played him before releasing him in the summer of 2020. The Nuggets signed him in November, 2020, and then traded him four months later with 2 2nd round picks for a washed-up JaVale McGee. Hartenstein finally got playing time in Cleveland, and in the summer of 2021 he signed with the Clippers as a free agent for the NBA minimum of $1.7 million.

Hartenstein had a successful season in Los Angeles, and the Knicks signed him that summer to a 2-year/ $16 million contract. He was deployed with Mitch Robinson as the Knicks center combo. New York had two successful seasons with Hartenstein, and they wanted to re-sign him, but they were well over the salary cap that summer. Meanwhile, the Thunder had a center problem, and a lot of cap room with which to solve it.

Sam Presti offered Hartenstein a deal he couldn't refuse- $87 million over 3 years. He had barely made it in the NBA, and now he would have one of the 50 highest salaries in the league. The Knicks couldn't come close to matching the offer. It would have made him their 3rd highest-paid player, and would have been more than their star player Jalen Brunson received in salary.

The Thunder were able to pay him because many of their players were still on rookie contracts, and they would be on those cheap deals for the 2026 season as well. Starting in the summer of 2026 that won't be the case, and the Thunder were projected to be way over the cap. Hartenstein was signed with the intention of being released after the 2026 season. But will the Thunder let him go? He was really good at basketball, and really important to the team. As Sam Presti would describe Hartenstein (and Caruso) after the season, "Their personalities were so well suited for our particular team… Elite role players that love being role players."

The Thunder picked up a new center, Thomas Sorber, in the 2025 draft, hoping to develop him to replace Hartenstein, but anything could happen. And Hartenstein was used to defying expectations.

(Update: "anything" did happen. Thomas Sorber, the Thunder's rookie center, tore his ACL in a summer workout and will miss the entire 2026 season. Hartenstein just became even more indispensable.)

Dec 29th in OKC. Win vs Grizzlies 130-106.

Memphis was flying high in 2nd place in the West behind the Thunder. The Grizzlies were playing without Ja Morant, but even with him there was a gulf of quality between the two teams, and it showed through in this game. The Thunder went on a 30-9 run with 7:30 left in the 2nd quarter, making 12 of their 15 shots and finding no resistance from Memphis. Memphis recorded two turnovers and suffered 3 blocks and 2 steals during this game-ending run, and the Thunder led by 26 points at halftime. JJJ shot 3-of-17, and Memphis had 21 turnovers that led to 31 Thunder points.

Gil Goose was only needed for 28 minutes, but he still scored 35 points on 14-of-19 shooting, and added 4 blocks. J-Dub had 14 points, 10 rebounds, and 8 assists, and Wiggins, Joe, Ajay, and Kenrich all scored in double-figures.

Kenrich Williams

Kenrich Williams went undrafted in 2018, but he received a professional contract from the New Orleans Pelicans. He started 47 games while averaging over 22 minutes per game in his first two seasons. In November of 2020, just before the 2021 season began (thanks, Covid), Kenrich was sent to OKC in the Jrue Holiday/Steven Adams trade. The Thunder was after draft picks in exchange for Adams, and Kenrich was only thrown in to help make the salaries match up.

It was a fortunate turn of luck, as Kenrich had proved to be a very useful player for the Thunder. He only started 31 games over the last 5 seasons, but he was a winning basketball player. Sam Presti understood his contributions, and Kenrich was rewarded with a 4-year/$27 million contract in the summer of 2022. The Thunder was in the middle of two tank seasons, but Kenrich was a player that Presti wanted around to help accelerate his rebuild.

Kenrich Williams could guard bigs, was good at defense, and was a good passer. He could shoot, too. He was a solid, fundamental player, and his best trait was making smart basketball decisions and winning plays. He knew when to pass and when to shoot, where he needed to be, and how to fit in with the other four guys on the floor. Kenrich was the type of player that can feel what all the other nine players were doing on the court.

Kenrich didn't play in every game because OKC's roster was so deep, but Coach Daigneault trusted him. He was always a plus on the floor when called upon. Kenrich was a solid rotation player on a low-cost contract. This was crucial in the salary cap era. He was a player that a team with no depth, like the Nuggets, would kill to have.

Dec 31st in OKC. Win vs Minnesota 113-105.

New Year's Eve Thunder games were an Oklahoma City tradition. The Timberwolves were a team with title aspirations, and they had a chip on their shoulders. The Wolves led by 6 points at halftime, but the Thunder went on a 36-10 run over the last 8 minutes of the 3rd quarter to take control of the game. The Thunder run was pushed along by a glorious stretch when the Wolves turned the ball over on 6 their 8 possessions.

However, for maybe the first time all season, an opponent was able to fight their way back. OKC was in control at 101-87 with 8:04 left in the game, but Minnesota went on a 3-14 run. The Wolves made 5 of their 9 shots, while OKC missed 7 of their 8 shots, and the Thunder lead was shrunk down to 104-101 with 3:14 to go. After Anthony Edwards made a couple of free throws to make it 106-103 with 2:03

left, Gil Goose hit a 3-pointer to put the lead back up to 6 points. Jaden McDaniels missed a 3, and on the next possession J-Dub stole the ball from Naz Reid. He took it down the court for a breakaway dunk to put the game away, and sent the happy crowd celebrating out into the New Year's Eve night.

Gil Goose closed the door on his spectacular 2024 with 40 points while shooting 15-of-23. The Thunder had 16 steals, led by Goose and Cason (who was in the starting lineup) with 4 steals each.

Jan 2nd in OKC. Win vs Clippers 116-98.

The Clippers came to town without Kawhi Leonard or James Harden. Still, they had a strong start. They led by 8 points after the 1st quarter and by 4 at halftime. Although Norm Powell missed 10 of his 11 shots and scored just 6 points, the Clippers got production from unsung players like Amir Coffey, who led LA with 26 points.

The Thunder put an end to the Clippers' 1st half optimism, starting the 2nd half with a 23-8 run to put the game out of reach. After another good performance, I texted my friends, "Ajay is such an awesome 2nd round pick."

Jan 3rd in OKC. Win vs NY Knicks 117-107.

This marked the start of a huge three-game stretch against the best teams in the Eastern Conference. I had these dates circled on my calendar for a while. The Thunder had passed every test this season. It was time for the Thunder to show the world who they were.

OKC was on a 13-game winning streak, but the Knicks were on a 9-game winning streak themselves to put them in 3rd place in their conference. The Knicks' coach Thibs famously didn't like to sub his players, and he played all five of his starters over 40 minutes. The Knicks were beating the Thunder by 14 points in the 1st half.

The Knicks were still up with 6:10 remaining, 92-97, when the Thunder went on a 25-10 run to finish the game. Aaron Wiggins led the comeback. He hit 3 3-pointers and had an and-one play in the last 6 minutes to put the dagger in. The Thunder shot a blazing 14-of-27 from 3, and Wiggins scored 15 of his 19 points in the 4th quarter.

It was an impressive win, and I remembered saying that the Knicks had played as well as they could have played, and they still lost. The Thunder had shown that they were the better team.

Unfortunately, this would be Ajay Mitchell's last game for months, as he was carrying a toe injury that required surgery. Although he returned for the playoffs, his promising rookie season was derailed. I had jinxed the poor guy with my text praise the very night before.

Jan 5th in OKC. Win vs Celtics 105-92.

Boston was the defending NBA champion, and they were in 2nd place in the East with 26 wins and 9 losses on the season. The Celtics were playing with their full team against OKC, ready to prove that they were still the top dog. And they started the game hot, scoring 65 points in the 1st half for a 10-point lead.

Coach Daigneault rode with his starters in this game, with Dort, Goose, Hartenstein, J-Dub, and Cason all playing at least 34 minutes. Just like in the previous three games, the Thunder turned a halftime deficit against a really good team into a come-from-behind win.

OKC cranked up their defensive intensity against the Celtics in the 2nd half, holding Boston to just 27 points on 20% shooting. Jaylen Brown didn't score a single point in the 2nd half, and the Celtics missed 21 of their 24 3-point attempts. Gil Goose scored 33 points and 11 rebounds in the game, and Wiggins added 15 points in just 20 minutes off the bench. I texted out, "I love how the Thunder go down, and instead of worry, I just think 'I wonder how they will win this one?'" OKC had just dispatched two of its title rivals. My confidence in the team could not have been higher.

Jan 8th in Cleveland. Loss vs Cavs 122-129.

The long-awaited clash of the NBA's top two teams was finally here. The Cavaliers stood at 31-4, and were on a 10-game winning streak. The Thunder, at 30-5, boasted a 15-game winning streak of their own. The last time two NBA teams with double-digit win streaks met was in 1995. This was as big of an occasion as a regular season game could be.

Both Oklahoma City and Cleveland put on a show, and the game stayed very close. The lead changed between the teams 30 times (!). OKC was without Caruso, Chet, and Ajay, so Coach Daigneault played a 9-man rotation with Cason starting. The Cavalier big men had monster stat lines- Mobley finished with 21 points and 10 rebounds, and Jarrett Allen had 25 points and 11 rebounds. The Thunder's big man, Frankenstein, also had a huge game with 18 points, 11 rebounds, and 8 assists. Donovan Mitchell, the Cavs' star, was Dorted, as he shot 3-of-16 for just 11 points.

Both teams played at a high level, and they kept scoring back and forth, matching each other blow for blow. The score was 112-114 with 5:37 left, 114-116 with 5:08 left, 118-121 with 3:44 remaining, 120-123 with 2:33 left... neither team could find an edge.

The pivotal play finally happened with the score 122-124 and just 1:39 left on the clock. Darius Garland missed a 3-pointer for Cleveland, but Jarrett Allen got the offensive rebound and was fouled. Allen made the first free throw and missed the second, but Cleveland gathered the offensive rebound. Donovan Mitchell then missed a jump shot, but Cleveland got the offensive rebound again. Mobley then missed a 3-pointer, but Cleveland got yet another offensive rebound, and Mobley finally made a jump shot for Cleveland. Their lead was now up to 5 points with just 1:07 left, and the game was over.

It was a disappointing finish, because Cleveland was allowed to rebound four consecutive misses with the game on the line. But it was also encouraging, because OKC was clearly just as good of a team as Cleveland was.

This was the week that the Thunder ran the gauntlet and showed that they were the favorites to win the championship. Oklahoma City felled the red-hot Knicks, trounced the defending champion Celtics, and in Cleveland they proved that they were every bit as good as the Cavaliers. There was no team in the NBA for Oklahoma City to be afraid of.

Well, except the Dallas Mavericks...

Jan 10th in NYC. Win vs Knicks 126-101.

The Knicks were upset after losing to the Thunder during previous week, and they couldn't wait to get them to Madison Square Garden for some revenge. Just kidding, New York actually just completely rolled over in this game. OKC was ahead 70-43 at halftime, and Knicks were 4-of-31 (13%) from 3 for the game. Mikal Bridges had an amazingly terrible stat line of 0 points and 1 rebound in 32 minutes. The Thunder shot 52% from 3, and they had 9 blocks and 9 steals. Isaiah Joe scored 31 points, and J-Will secured 10 rebounds in just 15 minutes. Goose lit up NYC for 39 points.

This concluded a stretch of 9 Thunder games in which 8 of their opponents would make the 2025 playoffs. The Thunder took on team after team of the best squads in the NBA, including the best four teams in the Eastern Conference, and dominated them with 8 wins and 1 loss. It would be the defining three weeks of the entire regular season for them. My opinion had shifted. I used to think OKC was an interesting contending team. Now, I expected them to win the title.

Jan 12th in DC. Win vs the Wizards 136-95.

It was nice for the Thunder to be able to take a night off versus the Wizards after such a brutal stretch of games over the holidays. OKC went on a 24-6 run that started in the 1st quarter, and were up

67-43 at halftime. OKC had eclipsed 100 points before the 3rd quarter ended, despite Gil Goose shooting just 5-of-17. Oklahoma City's excellent defense kept their opponent under 100 points for the 17th time in 38 games.

Coach Daigneault appeared to have chosen Cason Wallace as his fifth starter. He also settled on a nine-man rotation, with J-Will, Kenrich, Joe, and Wiggins coming off the bench. Caruso would also be in the rotation whenever he returned from what was ailing him. Chet and Ajay were out long-term. Wiggins had another big game with 23 points and 9 rebounds.

Aaron Wiggins

Aaron Wiggins was an afterthought as the 55th pick in the 2021 draft after his junior season in college. A 6'5" wing player, he had raised his game every season as a pro, and had played his way into being a solid rotation piece and occasional starter for the team. He had joined the Thunder at the perfect time. Wiggins benefited by delivering the two things that Sam Presti wanted during his rookie season- NBA experience for young players, and lots of losses. Our misery was Wiggins' gain, as he regularly started that season and was able to get plenty of playing time. I wasn't very impressed, and I didn't think he would last long on the Thunder. Wiggins shot just 30% on 3's that year, which definitely wouldn't work. I also thought he played hesitantly and timidly. But, for a late 2nd round pick, it was a very successful season. The Thunder then converted his 2-way contract into a regular NBA deal.

The next season, the Thunder made big roster improvements with key additions. As a result, playing time became much harder to come by. Wiggins definitely wasn't a starter anymore, but he did remain a trusted contributor, playing in 70 games. He was utilized if he was available, and his 3-point shooting improved all the way to 39% to became an asset now, not a liability.

Also, at some point in 2023, Wiggins became very aggressive with the ball. It was as if Coach Daigneault sat him down and told him this was his chance in the NBA, and he was blowing it. Instead of fitting in with the offense, Wiggins now was the offense. When he got the ball, he was shooting it if he was open. If he was covered, his head would go down and he would drive to the basket for a shot or a foul. It was a very direct style of play, and it was very effective with the Thunder's other players twisting the opposing defense around. By the time Wiggins got the ball, as a third option, the defense was scrambling, and he could exploit the chaos. Wiggins had seized his NBA dream, and he would keep improving.

In 2024, Wiggins was again a key rotation member, playing in 78 games and shooting 49% from 3. 49% on 3-pointers was absolutely elite, and it would have led the league by a mile if he had shot enough to qualify. He scored in double-figures 19 times, and played in all ten games in the playoffs, including the Game 1 win against Dallas when he scored 16 points. Wiggins signed a new 5-year contract after the 2024 season.

In 2025, Wiggins continued his ascendance, with his scoring average way up to 12 points per game, while starting 26 times in 76 games. He was very confident, and he shot 38% from 3-point range. Wiggins would score over 15 points in 23 games in 2025, including games of 41, 35, and 30 points. That 41-point game happened on February 1st, and it started a streak of 14 straight games with Wiggins scoring in double-figures.

How would Wiggins look as the primary or secondary scorer on a different team? I'm not sure he could be successful in that position, but he has done it well when the Thunder rest their stars. He also has improved every year. Will he stick with the Thunder in the years to come? It was tough to say. There was already a lot of competition for minutes, and players will be rotated out of the team as new players are drafted. But he was on a team-friendly contract, and he would be tough to replace.

Wiggins had a specific job on the team as offensive sparkplug, and he filled it well.

Jan 14th in Philly. Win vs 76ers 118-102.

This should have been an easy win- the 76ers were 15 and 22, and they were missing their star players Joel Embiid, Tyrese Maxey, and Boy George. The Thunder shot 56% for the game, and led 37-21 after one quarter. However, the 76ers fought back, and had the lead down to 91-87 with under 10 minutes to go before an 8-0 Thunder run ended their comeback bid. Did the Thunder almost lose to this ragtag Philly group because they were looking forward to their next game?

Jan 16th in OKC. Win vs Cleveland 134-114.

Oklahoma City got revenge in a rematch between the NBA's two best teams. Playing at home this time, the Thunder's statement win was never close. The Thunder led 32-14 after 1 quarter, and they used a 30-2 run to lead 75-49 at the break. OKC did not let up in the 3rd quarter, and the score was 119-81 when the 4th quarter started.

Donovan Mitchell was Dorted into 3-of-15 shooting for 8 points. Evan Mobley only had 5 points and 3 rebounds. None of the four Cavalier stars played over 24 minutes before the game was out of reach and they were rested. The NBA's two best teams were now tied at the top of the standings at 34 wins and 6 losses.

Hartenstein was out with a calf strain, so J-Will started at center for the Thunder. Gil Goose continued his immaculate play with 40 points and 8 assists. Lu Dort added 22 points on offense to his devastation of Donovan Mitchell on the defensive end. Even Brandon Carlsen had a night, scoring 11 points for the Thunder.

My friends and I were excited. I posted on our text thread, "Great performance. I will be disappointed if we don't win the title. The bar is so high." Brad responded, "If this team stays healthy, I don't see anyone who can beat us in a 7-game series." I pointed out, "This team is so awesome in every way," but then I asked, "So what is the Thunder's biggest weakness? If I was nitpicking, they have some problems creating without Gil Goose on the floor."

40 Game Summary

The Thunder had 9 wins and 1 loss in their last 10 games. They were now 7 games ahead of the 2nd place Houston Rockets, and running away with the Western Conference. OKC had proven they can beat everyone in the NBA, including the Cavaliers. They had just come through the hardest part of the schedule, and did so by winning 19 of their previous 20 games. Their rotation was settled, and

Jalen Williams was headed to his first All-Star game. Gil Goose was absolutely dominating the league.

OKC was a very deep team, with two of the best players in the world, followed by 10 other very good players. The Thunder was much better around the basket compared to last season, and their defense was historically outstanding. They could play big or small, slow or fast. And this still wasn't the best version of the 2025 Thunder, because Chet Holmgren was out of action.

Brad was right. With the season half over, the only thing that could stop the Thunder was injuries.

Or the Dallas Mavericks...

Jan 17th in Dallas. Loss vs Mavs 98-106.

Dallas didn't have Luka Doncic, and PJ Washington played more like himself with 16 points and 7 rebounds, but Dallas still beat OKC. OKC was without Gil Goose (sprained wrist) and Hartenstein, so Wiggins and J-Will started, and J-Dub was in charge of running the offense.

Dallas outscored OKC 17-41 in the 2nd quarter to give them a 20-point lead at halftime. OKC bounced back in the 3rd, closing the gap to just one point. This set the stage for an exciting 4th quarter. Dallas was ahead 91-92 with 4:35 left. Then, on three of the next four Thunder possessions, J-Dub missed a step-back 3-pointer, committed an offensive foul, and missed another step-back 3. This allowed Dallas to increase their lead to 7 points. J-Dub then hit a jumper, but he followed that with a missed jump shot with 1:07 left. Dallas then fouled J-Dub with 43 seconds left, and he made both free throws to bring the score to 95-101. On the next play, however, he got his layup attempt blocked by PJ, and then was handed a technical foul for arguing the play. It wasn't a great display by Jalen Williams as OKC's primary ballhandler, or a good omen with SGA missing his first game of the year.

Dallas was just the worst.

Jan 19th in OKC. Win vs Brooklyn 127-101.

This game against the 14-28 Nets was just about over before it started. The Thunder used an 18-0 run in the 1st quarter to go up 39-19, during which time they shot 9-of-13 on 3-pointers. The blazing hot start continued for the rest of the game, with the Thunder shooting 44% on 3's and 55% overall. Goose had 27 points, 10 assists, and 4 steals in 29 minutes, and Isaiah Joe ended up with 24 points on 8 3-pointers.

J-Dub sat out due to a hip injury. He joined Hartenstein, Kenrich, and Chet in street clothes. This meant Joe and J-Will were in the starting lineup. J-Will was backed up by Ousmane Dieng, who got 12 points. Gil Goose sat for the entire 4th quarter for the 4th time in 5 games. The win officially secured Coach Daigneault's place as the All-Star game head coach.

Jan 22nd in OKC. Win vs Utah Jazz 123-114.

This was somehow a very close game against the team with the worst record in the Western Conference. The Thunder were missing Hartenstein and Chet, so the Jazz outrebounded OKC 52-39 with 23 (!) offensive rebounds. All five Jazz starters scored in double-figures for a balanced offense, and the Thunder lead was only 2 points at halftime.

The Jazz ultimately were undone by 15 steals and 27 total turnovers which led to 39 Thunder points. The game was tied 106-106 with 5:26 left when the Thunder went on an 11-0 run to close it out. J-Dub started the run with an and-one, then Lu Dort fought for an offensive rebound after a Thunder miss, which led to a Cason 3-pointer. A minute later, Gil Goose got an offensive rebound off his own missed 3-pointer. This led to Goose hitting a 3. A Caruso steal led to two more points from Goose. OKC led by 11 with 2:53 to go, and the Jazz couldn't get back in the game.

Gil Goose

Shai Gilgeous-Alexander scored a career-high 54 points in the game, his latest highlight in this MVP season. SGA was undoubtedly the superstar of this Oklahoma City team. He had already exceeded every expectation any Oklahoman could have had for him, while comporting himself without reproach.

SGA had no flaws in his game. Defensively, he was immense. He stole the ball at an elite clip, but that stat wasn't necessarily a good indication of defensive talent. It can be manipulated by players who take bad risks. I spent years watching Russ dive in, ill-advised, for long-shot steals. Gil Goose did not do that. He was a legitimate above-average one-on-one defender, as well as an elite help defender. Goose was too strong to overpower, too quick to dribble by, and too long to shoot over. He was great at blocking shots from the weakside, and also great at poking the ball away from the backside.

Offense, of course, was SGA's specialty. Goose was unstoppable with the ball. He could shoot 3's (over 37% in 2025 on a high volume), and he loved to step back into those shots. Goose was so quick on his drive that defenders had to backpedal. This allowed him to stop and elevate for wide-open midrange jump shots. He made an amazing 53% of those shots from 10-to-16 feet in 2025. Goose also was strong enough to post up on the wings, and he unveiled a Micheal Jordan baseline fallback shot in 2025. It made me love him even more.

SGA's arms were so long that his shot was nearly impossible to block. He also had mastered a push off to create space on his drives. Pushing off was illegal, but Goose used his chest and a teeny bit of his elbow to do it, instead of extending his arm. If a defender stayed with him on the push off, Goose could fall back for a shot. If his defender bit on the fall back, Goose would step underneath or 360 around him. His balance was impeccable. He could not be stopped.

The only way to contain SGA was to double or triple-team him. But that was no answer, either. OKC surrounded Goose with elite shooters, and teams could not give them wide-open shots and expect to win. Plus, Goose was an elite AND willing passer. He loved to drive all the way in to the basket, get all the defenders in the air, and pass out to his teammates for open 3-pointers. SGA did not hog the ball, and he was happy to pass up a game-ending shot if it was the right play. We Oklahomans had spent years watching Durant and Westbrook take all of the shots down the stretch. The difference between our new superstar and them was jarring.

Dribble drives were Goose's specialty, more so than all of his other substantial skills. He had a quick first step, and could always initiate a drive with or without a pick. SGA could cross opponents over, or just use his body to ride a player to the hoop. He could finish in every way- left hand, right hand, bank shot, one-handed scoop shot, over shot-blockers, under shot-blockers. Goose was great at finishing on the opposite side of the rim. SGA's arms were so long that he could just put the ball into an area where the defenders weren't at before flipping it in. He was able to continuously bait the defenders into fouling him, and he had made over 80% of his attempts from the free throw line every season in his career.

In a short 17 years, we Oklahomans have been blessed by three superstar Hall of Fame players. Kevin Durant actually was similar to SGA in many ways. Both of them were so lanky that almost any shot was an open shot. Both were excellent finishers at the rim, and both loved pulling up into jump shots. Durant and Goose were consistent threats for the scoring title and MVP crown, and both of them were All-NBA 1st team regulars. But Durant could never come close to the ball-handling skills or driving ability of SGA.

Westbrook and Goose couldn't be more different. Russ lived to punish opponents, and loved to out-physical them and out-tough them. His game was always violent, based on his elite speed and power. Russ was always going head-on into bigger players, looking to prove to everyone that he was the best and the baddest player on the court. I imagine that Russ believed a perfect game would be one where he had 50 dunks in a row.

Goose was all finesse. He hardly ever dunked (54 total in 2025), preferring to look for a way around his opponents. If he got stopped temporarily by his defender, he would just begin another sequence of moves.

Shai also had a gravitas and such a cool demeanor. His teammates were so goofy, while he was their leader gliding above their nonsense. But unlike Jordan and Kobe, Goose was not cruel. He genuinely loved his teammates, and he considered them to be his peers. And he signed hours of autographs for the fans. Goose was just an impeccable individual. We were so lucky to have him.

And it was also luck that got him to the Thunder in the first place. Doc Rivers, a coach famous for not playing rookies, put Gil Goose in his starting lineup in his first season in 2019. Goose averaged 26 minutes and only 10 points per game, but the Clippers fought hard against including him in the Paul George trade. But Sam Presti was insistent. I, and most people, didn't see what those GMs saw, but the professionals were obviously right.

Goose joined a 2020 Oklahoma City team that was led by veterans Chris Paul, Steven Adams, Danilo Gallinari, and Dennis Schroder. He fit in well with his teammates, and he raised his scoring average to 19 points per game. However, he wasn't their key player that season.

Presti sent OKC into full tanking mode in 2021, trading away all the Thunder's veterans. The team was turned over to Goose. But Goose was too skilled for a tanking team, as he scored over 23 points and dished 6 assists per game. More importantly, he helped the Thunder achieve a 19-24 record, good for 12th in the Western Conference. Presti wanted his team to be last place, so Goose was forced to end his 3rd season after the Thunder's 43rd game. The Thunder said it was due to a "plantar fascia tear" in his foot, but I was skeptical about any OKC injury report. The Thunder finished the season by losing 26 of their final 29 games without SGA.

2022 was another tank year for Presti and the Thunder. Presti had a difficult balancing act to maneuver through. He wanted to lose every game, but he also wanted to further SGA's development. Goose averaged over 24 points a game in 2022, but OKC was really bad. SGA randomly missed 5 of the first 48 games of the season, and the Thunder lost all 5 of them. Their record was 14-34 at that point, and they were tied for last place in the Western Conference. Gil Goose then hurt his ankle, forcing him to miss 10 games, and OKC went 4-6. Goose returned for the next 12 games, and the team went 2-10. He then re-injured his ankle and missed 11 of the last 12 games. OKC went 4-8 to finish at 24-58, good for the 4th worst record in the NBA.

After four seasons as a pro, Goose obviously had talent, but he hadn't taken over the world. The Thunder had given him the keys to the offense for two years, but he had only played 91 games, while missing 63 games. And the Thunder's winning percentage had only been .300.

Gil Goose exploded in his 5th year. He averaged over 31 points per game and led OKC to a successful season. He was an efficient scorer too, making 51% of his shots and 90% of his free throws. The accolades poured in. Goose made the All-Star team, was 1st team All-NBA, and was voted as the 5th Most Valuable Player in the league.

2024 was an even better year for Goose. He scored 30 points per game and led Oklahoma City to the best record in the Western Conference. Goose again made the All-Star team and was 1st team All-NBA. He finished runner-up to Nikola Jokic for the Most Valuable Player award.

2025 would be Gil Goose's best year yet. He won the scoring title by averaging almost 33 points a game, and he won his first MVP award. Oklahoma City would have one of the greatest seasons in NBA history behind Goose's play and leadership. And he was still very young at just 27 years-old. His Oklahoma City legacy hasn't topped Kevin

Durant's, yet. But I have no doubt he will be remembered as the Thunder's greatest ever player. And hopefully he'll have multiple championships as well.

Jan 23rd in OKC. Loss vs Dallas Mavs 115-121.

Luka the Fat missed yet another game against the Thunder, and it again didn't matter. Dallas won the close game, as PJ Washington the God had 22 points and 19 rebounds. Dallas shot 53% from field goals and 45% from 3's.

The Thunder were missing Hartenstein, Joe, Chet, and Ajay. They used a nine-man rotation, with J-Dub, Goose, Dort, Cason and J-Will starting. Caruso, Wiggins, Kenrich, and Dillon Jones came off the bench.

Dallas had the game in hand in the 3rd quarter, up by 13, before the Thunder slowly came back. Goose hit a jumper with 5:29 left, making it 100-102. But Quentin Grimes quickly answered with a 3-pointer for Dallas. OKC's last chance came when Gil Goose made a tough layup with 1:21 left, bringing the score to 106-110. Then, Caruso stole the ball from Kyrie as he went up for a layup. But Goose missed a 3-pointer after the turnover with 1:02 left, and Dallas made their free throws to close out the game.

I wish Dallas would just leave us alone.

Jan 26th in Portland. Win vs Blazers 118-108.

Isaiah Hartenstein returned to help OKC to a 52-22 advantage in points in the paint, but Portland made 18 of their 40 3-pointers to stay in the game. The Thunder outscored Portland 39-26 in the 2nd quarter for a 13-point halftime lead. However, the Blazers started the 4th quarter strong. They scored the first 10 points, trimming a 15-point Thunder lead to just 93-88 in under 3 minutes. The Thunder then responded with a 12-2 run of their own, devastating Portland with 4 3-pointers, 4 offensive rebounds, and 3 charges drawn. The Thunder lead was back up to 15, and the game was over.

Jan 29th in SF. Loss to Warriors 109-116.

OKC lost again to this proud but fading Warriors team, as OKC only shot 23% from 3-point range on 39 attempts. The Thunder had a 10-point lead at halftime, and benefited from a magnificent 52-point game from Gil Goose, but the game turned with OKC leading 93-92 with 9:00 minutes to play. Oklahoma City went ice cold, only scoring 5 points over the next 6 minutes, and Golden State took the lead 98-106. OKC made a comeback with less than 3 minutes left, starting as J-Dub hit a 3-pointer. Dennis Schroder then turned the ball over on a charge, and J-Dub followed it with a layup to close the gap to just 3 points. But Steph Curry ended all hope with a classic Steph Curry dagger 3-pointer, and the game wasn't close again. Andrew Wiggins scored 27 points, and even Kevon Looney somehow had 18 points (his next highest scoring game of the entire season was 12 points).

Feb 1st in OKC. Win vs Kings 144-110.

Sacramento was hammered by the Thunder, who outscored the Kings 46-24 in the 2nd quarter to take a 27-point lead at halftime. The Kings were outrebounded by a massive margin of 70-37, and the Thunder shot 41% from 3. Gil Goose had 29 points and 9 assists before sitting out the 4th quarter again. J-Dub and Caruso didn't play, and Cason got injured in the game, so Dieng got to play 25 minutes.

The biggest story in the game was Aaron Wiggins going crazy for 41 points and 14 rebounds. His teammates kept feeding him the ball at the end of the game to get him past 40. There was a big celebration during the postgame interview for the game of his career.

Feb 3rd in OKC. Win vs Milwaukee 125-96.

OKC crushed Milwaukee in a revenge game for their loss in the NBA Cup Final. Milwaukee sat every good player they had, including Johnny Boy, Damian Lillard, Bobby Portis, Brook Lopez, and Kris Middleton. J-Dub was out again along with Caruso and Cason, so Kenrich and Wiggins started. OKC was up 78-44 at halftime, and led by 41 after 3 quarters. OKC dominated in the paint, outscoring the Bucks 62-36 and outrebounding them 55-37.

Gil Goose went an unstoppable 9-of-11 for 21 points in the 1st quarter alone, and he finished with 34 points in just 23 minutes. Ousmane Dieng burned Milwaukee up with 21 points, 8 rebounds, and 5 assists, and Isaiah Joe added 18 points in the blowout win.

The Luka Doncic Trade

The big news of the day broke that morning. The world woke up to the seismic news that the Dallas Mavericks had parted ways with their generational talent, Luka Doncic. Dallas had smoked OKC for 2 seasons in a row. After beating OKC 146-111 in February 2024, Dallas then crushed the top-seeded Thunder in the 2024 playoffs, winning four of the last five games. And Dallas should have also won the one game that they lost to OKC in that stretch.

The Mavs continued to dominate Oklahoma City during the 2025 season. OKC's record versus Dallas in 2025 was 1 win and 3 losses. OKC's record vs the rest of the NBA was 67-11. Dallas was the only team the Thunder should fear, and they were no longer a problem.

It probably was the craziest trade ever. Doncic was undeniably one of the very best basketball players in the world. He had already made 5 (!) All-NBA 1st teams by the time he was 25 years-old. (For comparison, SGA just made his third All-NBA 1st team in 2025. And Goose is 8 months older than Doncic.)

Doncic was also a serial winner. He led Real Madrid to the Euroleague championship at just 18 years-old in 2018 (He also won the Euroleague MVP that year.) He then dragged a mediocre 52-win Mavericks team to the Western Conference Finals in 2022 as their 23-year-old star. Doncic took another mediocre 50-win Dallas team all the way to the 2024 NBA Finals as a 25-year-old. Nico Harrison said that he traded Doncic because he wanted Dallas to win. But winning was all that Doncic had ever done.

Players that good and that successful just don't get traded. And to make the transaction completely unbearable, the Mavs only offered to trade Luka to the Lakers, shutting out offers from the other 28 teams. And in return for Doncic, Dallas only received one 1st round pick and Anthony Davis, a 31-year-old center who had spent much of his career injured. And as soon as Davis got to Dallas, he picked up an injury that kept him out for weeks. Never before has the phrase "adding insult to injury" been so apropos (although in this case it was "injury to insult").

Dallas could have gotten a way better deal, without question. According to ESPN, five teams (Oklahoma City, Brooklyn, New Orleans, San Antonio, and Orlando) could have offered Dallas multiple players PLUS at least five (!) 1st round picks for Luka. I think all five would have done it, too. San Antonio made a huge trade that very same day for DeAaron Fox. And Orlando traded a ton of 1st round picks for Desmond Bane after the season. Either of those teams would have way preferred to have Doncic instead. Neither Fox nor Bane will ever be anywhere close to as good as Luka. Brooklyn and New Orleans have been praying for years for a lifeline like Luka would have provided them. Only OKC would have been a question mark, considering their team chemistry and the fact that they were already really good. I still think Presti would have done it, though. Doncic was one of the most special players in NBA history, and adding him to your team guaranteed a certain base level of success.

Dallas supposedly jettisoned Doncic because he was out of shape, he was not good enough on defense, and he liked to drink too much. These all were flimsy excuses, and not just to me, but to the world. Nico Harrison should be held criminally negligent for the trade. Instead, he kept his GM job plus whatever amount of money the Lakers must have paid him under the table. Importantly to our story, the Mavericks had just removed themselves as arguably the biggest obstacle in the Thunder's path to winning the title. This "improved" Dallas team wouldn't even make the playoffs.

Feb 5th in OKC. Win vs Phoenix 140-109.

Gil Goose ended up with another great game of 50 points, while Kevin Durant again skipped out on playing in Oklahoma City. The Suns were a .500 team after this loss, but their players had nearly given up. They ended the season with only 11 more wins and 21 more losses. Their indifference showed, as they let OKC dominate in the paint with a 17-3 advantage in offensive rebounds and 62-32 in points. The Thunder drove to the basket at will.

The Thunder started the 3rd quarter down by 2 points, but the OKC defensive pressure destroyed the Suns over the next 12 minutes. The Thunder scored the first 13 points of the second half, and built a 25-point lead heading into the 4th quarter. OKC shot 15-of-25 for the quarter, while Phoenix went 1-of-13 with 6 turnovers off of 5 Thunder steals and 3 Thunder blocks. It was yet another dominant Thunder display in a 3rd quarter to win a game.

Feb 7th in OKC. Win vs Toronto 121-109.

Although the Thunder only won by 11 points, this game was never in doubt. The Thunder were up by 11 at halftime, and Toronto only stayed close because they made 19 of their 41 3-pointers. But the Raptors couldn't stop Oklahoma City from getting to the basket, with the Thunder winning the points in the paint 60-to-34. Both Cason and Dort missed the game, so Wiggins started and provided 18 points.

The big news of the game was that, from out of nowhere, Chet Holmgren was back! Coach Daigneault put him directly into the starting lineup, and he had 4 blocks in just 22 minutes. Chet had missed the previous 40 games, and the Thunder could finally play their best lineups with his return to the team.

50 Game Summary

The All-Star break was almost here, and OKC was 41-9 in their first 50 games. Their latest ten-game stretch had started poorly. They had lost three straight to rivals, while only winning against three weaker lottery teams. OKC then responded to those poor results with 4 straight blowout wins. Gil Goose had furthered his MVP case during these 10 games by scoring at least 50 points on 3 different occasions. Isaiah Joe had multiple high-scoring games as well.

OKC was still in first place. Meanwhile, Houston had hit a rough patch, and they were now in 4th place. The Memphis Grizzlies were up to 2nd, 6.5 games behind OKC in the standings. And Dallas, previously our looming nemesis, had self-detonated their season. Anthony Davis had gotten injured on February 8th vs the Rockets, and he would miss six weeks. By the time he returned on March 25th, Dallas was in 11th place and doomed to miss the playoffs.

Feb 8th in Memphis. Win vs Grizzlies 125-112.

The Grizzlies had shot up into 2nd place in the Western Conference, and were playing at home with a chance to prove themselves against the Thunder. Things went poorly for them, and the game was never close. The Thunder led 69-52 at the half, and OKC had scored 104 points before the 4th quarter had even started.

Cason Wallace, Lu Dort, and Chet Holmgren all sat out, so Alex Caruso started. Caruso was responsible for Dorting Ja Morant into a 6-of-19 shooting performance. Aaron Wiggins also started, and he hit 8 3-pointers for 26 points to go with 11 rebounds.

These last five huge wins had me excited, as shown in a text barrage to my friends. "I've spent like 5 hours this week talking about how awesome the Thunder are. Maybe the best starting lineup in the NBA. 12 deep. I don't even know who our playoff closing lineup will be. There are 8 possible guys. Such good problems to have. I love our team. I love Kenrich. I love Ajay. And they'd be lucky to see the floor in the playoffs." My feelings were sincere, but I was also probably drunk. My poor friends, always having to put up with me.

Feb 10th in OKC. Win vs Pelicans 137-101.

The Thunder cruised past the miserable, last-place Pelicans for their 6th blowout victory in a row. The Thunder shot 49% from 3, and had 15 steals and 8 blocks, led by Chet with 5 blocks. The Pelicans were missing CJ McCollum, Dejounte Murray, and Herb Jones, so somebody named Matkovic played 32 minutes for them. Lu Dort returned for OKC after missing a couple of games.

The Thunder were up 72-50 at halftime, and they scored 102 points in the first three quarters. Aaron Wiggins continued his hot streak with 24 points in just 25 minutes. Goose had 31 points before sitting out the 4th quarter for the fourth time in six games.

Feb 12th in OKC. Win vs Miami Heat 115-101.

The 25-win, 26-loss Miami Heat made this game really tough, as the Thunder were down by 21 points in the 2nd quarter, and were losing 83-93 at the end of the 3rd. OKC turned it on in the 4th quarter, outscoring the Heat 32-8 to come back for the win. The Thunder started the 4th quarter with a 24-0 run that included 2 forced turnovers, 3 steals, and a blocked shot. The Heat only made 3 of their last 18 shots to end the game. I texted out, "Such a great Thunder win. A game like this just shows that they have 'it'."

Feb 13th in Minnesota. Loss vs Wolves 101-116.

The Thunder were on the road, playing the second night of back-to-back games. The All-Star break began after the game, and OKC had an 8-game lead in 1st place. The Thunder had no chance of caring about this game, and it showed. The Wolves were up 24-37 at the end of the 1st quarter, and it never was close afterwards.

Naz Reid had a 27-point, 14-rebound double-double. Terrance Shannon tormented the Thunder with 13 points and 6 rebounds. SGA was held under 25 points for the first time in 22 games, scoring 24 points on 6-of-21 shooting, although he did contribute 8 rebounds and 9 assists.

The All-Star Break

I'm going to use the All-Star break to highlight an important part of the 2025 Oklahoma City season - the team's goofy pregame and postgame routines. I hope they never get lost to the sands of time.

Many professional athletes had unique, superstitious pregame routines. For example, LeBron would grab fistfuls of talcum powder and toss it into the air. The Thunder were no different. My favorite part of their 2025 pregame routine was when Gil Goose was announced as the last starter. He went down the line, high-fiving his teammates. Then, he joined the other four starters in a circle to break out in a quick dance. I always take that as my invitation to join in with them to dance, whether I'm at the game or at a bar or in my living room. If I miss the player introductions at home, I'll rewind the broadcast so I can dance with the team and properly orient myself for the game.

The Thunder's sideline reporter, Nick Gallo, would come on the broadcast for his pregame report after we danced. When the camera started rolling, J-Will always came in behind Gallo to brush off his suit coat shoulders and tidy him up. J-Will then exited the scene, and J-Dub popped into the background to execute two Radio City Rockette-style toe-touch kicks. J-Dub then would move in close to rest his face on one of Nick's shoulders. He quickly switched to the other shoulder and then back again, and then he was out in a flash. It was ridiculous, and it was goofy, and I could never get enough of it.

Nick Gallo also interviewed a Thunder player after every game. Sideline interviews were almost universally boring, and the Thunder's were especially so.

I pictured Sam Presti hosting a week-long "interview school" at training camp. He would teach coaches and players how to deflect questions. Then, he'd have them memorize the only five acceptable answers for any media inquiry:

- Some form of "Just trying to play hard defense".
- Some form of "My teammates really helped me out".
- Some form of "Just trying to get better every day".
- Some form of "Just trying to keep making good plays".
- And, of course, "Just keep stacking games".

They watched Coach Daigneault's pregame interviews for a masterclass in using a lot of words to say nothing. Then Sam had Nick Gallo come in so all the players could practice one-on-one interviews. I envisioned Presti watching and critiquing their answers. Maybe a pop quiz or final exam was involved.

Then Presti would explain the punishments he would mete out to his players for letting any news of injuries or of anything negative to slip out. There was likely a bonus for the most boring interview, the most days saying "keep stacking days," or for the answer least related to the actual question.

So, what did these really young men, constrained by expectations and rules, do? They made the post-game interviews into a lovable, funny game. Nick Gallo said that Chet started it, but I remember it being Jaylin Williams. During an interview in late 2023 (I think), Jaylin Williams butted into the camera frame. He listened closely to his teammate, resting his chin on his hand, deep in contemplation. He nodded in agreement to whatever banality was being said. It was hilarious.

He came back to pretend to listen again at the next day's interview, and the next. Soon, more players were getting involved. It eventually became expected that most of the team, especially the rookies, had to be part of the post-game interview crew. Before long, just standing together with arms around shoulders wasn't enough. J-Dub started taking the microphone at the end of the interview and barking into it like a dog. But J-Dub wasn't the only team member who played like a tenacious dog. Soon, all the players were having to take their turn barking into the microphone to prove their doggedness. Even Nick Gallo was eventually peer-pressured into ending an interview by barking into the mic.

Then the interviews morphed again. The players always had towels around to dry off their sweat. Somebody, likely J-Will again, started toweling off the interview subject to annoy him mid-sentence. Then the interviews became a game of stacking towels on the interviewee. Shoulders, heads, just towel after towel, trying to break the interviewee's concentration.

No player was above getting the treatment. Gil Goose didn't get interviewed much by the local broadcast, because he usually was tapped for the national broadcasts. But even he would get the towels when it was his turn. But Goose also was the only player who could put an end to the shenanigans with a quick, knowing glance over at his cackling teammates.

After the towel treatment got old, the players turned their attention away from each other and onto Nick Gallo. He would get the full towel treatment every night towards the end of the 2025 season while trying to conduct his interviews in his suit and tie. But he wouldn't ever break. The players now had a challenge. They spent every postgame escalating the abuse on Nick. They tried to make him acknowledge their presence in any way.

It culminated at the season's end against Charlotte. The players dressed him in a Thunder warm-up top during his interview, with Chet holding the microphone so they could zip him up. Then, as he continued the interview, they added J-Will's jersey over his head. J-Dub adjusted the microphone to get his sleeves tidied up. They put the hoodie over his head and added a towel, and by the interview's end Nick Gallo was dressed like a

Thunder player. Everyone was laughing, including Nick.

A few games later, the players used the postgame interview to reveal a Nick Gallo t-shirt that they had commissioned. It had a montage of Nick getting dressed in the warm-up top. They all put on a t-shirt and danced around in celebration of a fun season.

Feb 21st in Utah. Win vs Jazz 130-107.

The Thunder returned from the All-Star break with Coach Daigneault pretty set on his starting lineup of Chet, J-Dub, Dort, Hartenstein, and Goose. Cason Wallace returned after missing the previous seven games with a shoulder strain. Utah was not a good team in 2025, fighting for last place with a record of 13-41. The Thunder easily handled them, shooting 44% on 3's and handing out ten blocked shots. The score was 68-47 at halftime, and the game was never close after that.

Feb 23rd in Minnesota. Win vs Wolves 130-123.

Minnesota started the game just 1-for-12 on 3-pointers, and they trailed by 12 points at the end of the 1st quarter. However, they went on a 24-4 run in the 2nd quarter to go up by 2 points at the half, despite not having Gobert or Randle and playing just a 7-man rotation. Oklahoma City shot 54% from 3 in the game, and led by 7 after 3 quarters, but

Minnesota took the lead back in the 4th. The Wolves were up 105-110 with 8 minutes left. Then, an 18-2 OKC run turned the game. Alex Caruso hit three 3-pointers and made a steal to lead the Thunder back to win. Anthony Edwards had 29 points, 10 rebounds and 7 assists for Minnesota, but Gil Goose had a bigger game with 37 points, 8 rebounds, and 8 assists.

Feb 24th in OKC. Loss vs Wolves 128-131 in OT.

The two rivals played again the very next day. Oklahoma City was blowing the game out until Terrance Shannon scored 11 points to lead a big Minnesota comeback in the 4th quarter to force overtime.

The Thunder was up 64-45 at halftime, and the 3rd quarter ended with Minnesota down by 22 points. However, the Wolves outscored the Thunder 19-41 in the final quarter. OKC did not score at all in the final 3:55 of the game. The Thunder still had a lead of 3 points with 18 seconds left when Jaden McDaniels missed a jump shot. The Wolves got the offensive rebound, and Caruso fouled McDaniels as he made a layup. His free throw tied the game, and Gil Goose missed a layup at the buzzer to win.

Our NBA text thread was blowing up. Jeff's mood was, "the Thunder look like s**t these last five minutes." I said, "Is this a 20-0 run? WTH? It was like 121-106 with under 3 minutes left?" Jeff said,

"We just kept jacking 3's," and I replied, "Well, this is frustrating."

The frustration continued as Minnesota won the overtime 7 to 10. OKC was down 128-129 at the end, and Gil Goose drove in for a layup with a chance to take the lead, but Anthony Edwards flew in from behind for a monster block. Goose had a 3-point opportunity at the buzzer to tie it after Minnesota had made their free throws with 6 seconds left, but his shot rimmed out.

Terrance Shannon ended up with 17 points and 10 rebounds for probably his best professional game ever, while Anthony Edwards provided 17 points, 13 rebounds, and 8 assists. Gil Goose also had a huge game with 39 points, 10 rebounds, and 8 assists. Brad texted us, "Bad Loss". It would end up being the second worst loss of the regular season for Oklahoma City. I replied, "The good news is this team so rarely has a bad game that those bad games really stick out."

Feb 26th in Brooklyn. Win vs Nets 129-121.

The Nets management badly wanted to tank their season, but the players had surprisingly kept them in the playoff race. In response, mysterious injuries had started happening, and their players recently began getting traded and released. The suddenly undistinguished Nets had a box score for this game that included Killian Hayes with 19 points (what?), Day'Ron Sharpe with 25 points and 15 rebounds (who?), and Zaire Williams with 18 points and 10 rebounds (what is even happening?). These anonymous Nets smashed OKC in the first half, scoring 76 points (!) and leading by 15.

This was one of the games that differentiated this Thunder squad from a good team to a historically excellent team. Coming off a tough loss, and well in control of 1st place, the Thunder should have quit. But they did not capitulate. Instead, they came back with a 27-7 run to open the 4th quarter, which included an 18-0 stretch where the Nets' 9 possessions ended with 5 missed 3-pointers, 3 steals, and a blocked shot.

Feb 28th in Atlanta. Win vs Hawks 135-119.

Oklahoma City went up 40-23 in the first quarter, and never trailed in the game. Atlanta got the score closer in the 2nd quarter, but OKC blew the game back out in the 3rd quarter with a 17-3 run in the last 4:51. They then coasted to victory. Isaiah Joe scored 12 quick points before hurting his back, and Chet only played 15 minutes with a calf strain. Caruso didn't play at all. Trae Young had 19 points and 12 assists, but he was Dorted into shooting 5-of-14, and Lu Dort added 20 points of his own on 6 made 3-pointers.

March 2nd in San Antonio. Win vs Spurs 146-132.

The Spurs had recently lost Victor Wembanyama for the season due to blood clots, having already lost Coach Popovich in November to a stroke. Our old friend Bismack Biyombo started for San Antonio! The Spurs played well in the first half, scoring 77 points while making 16 3-pointers (the NBA record was 18). Their halftime advantage was 5 points, but the Thunder started the 2nd half with a 13-4 run to take the lead as the Spurs went ice cold on their 3-point attempts (0-8 in the 3rd). The Spurs got the OKC lead down to 108-105 in the 4th quarter, but the Thunder slowly pulled away from there. Kenrich and Dort were ejected from the game for fighting with Julian Champagnie. J-Dub scored a career-high 41 points.

60 Game Summary

Oklahoma City now had 49 wins and 11 losses. The last 10 games had been a mixed bag. OKC had given up over 100 points in every game, and their last 5 opponents had all scored at least 119 points. The bad loss to the Wolves before the All-Star break was unusual because this Thunder team never took nights off. The 7 Thunder wins in a row before that Wolves game had mostly been blowouts, though.

The Thunder killed the Jazz after the All-Star Break, then had a tough win vs the Wolves followed up by a tough loss to the Wolves, and then a tough win against the Nets. OKC got back on track with huge scores against the Hawks and the Spurs.

The Thunder players were healthy, and the team was clicking. OKC has 1st place locked up with a 10.5 game lead over the 2nd place Lakers. What was there left to play for? Start the playoffs already.

March 3rd in OKC. Win vs Houston 137-128.

The opposing teams started resting their best players against OKC, throwing in the towel before the game even started. The Rockets had Alperen Sengun, Fred Van Vleet, Amen Thompson, and Dillon Brooks sit out this one. It still was a close game. OKC was only winning 112-106 with 8:43 left, but Houston missed five straight shots as the lead extended to 120-106, and Houston never got back in it.

Gil Goose scoring 28 first half points, and 51 points in total. I texted my friends, "I think this is the best Thunder team ever. Not the most talented, but definitely the best Thunder defense ever, and the best team. And most balanced. Hardly any weakness."

March 5 in Memphis. Win vs Grizzlies 120-103.

The game was close, but OKC won every quarter while shooting 42% from 3. Memphis had a chance with the score at 67-64 with 7:53 left in the 3rd quarter, but a 14-2 Oklahoma City run put an end to any of the Grizzlies' hopes. Ja Morant was Dorted into an 8-for-22 night, ending up with 24 points. Gil Goose had another huge game with 41 points and 8 assists.

March 7th in OKC. Win vs Portland 107-89.

Portland was a young team, but they actually were playing pretty well, as their record was 28-35. But OKC still won despite resting all their best players- Goose, J-Dub, Dort, Chet, Frankenstein, and Cason- and turning the game over to their bench players. Kenrich played 32 minutes, Dieng played 36 minutes, and J-Will ran the offense from the top of the key.

OKC was up by 18 points at the half, but Portland fought back to cut the OKC lead to 87-85 with 7:07 left in the game. The OKC bench players then broke the game open with a 20-4 run to end it, holding the Blazers to 1 made shot in their final 13. Aaron Wiggins had 30 points, OKC had 12 steals and 8 blocks, and J-Will showed his quality with a triple double of 10 points, 11 rebounds, and 11 assists. OKC's bench showed that they could play winning team basketball better than half of the league's starters could.

My friends and I were excited. Jeff texted, "God, I hope we win it all! This team loves one another more than any team I have ever seen. It is awesome!" I replied, "That game reminded me of a couple of years ago when we lost in the play-in (2023 season). They didn't have the talent, but they played hard and played well every game."

March 9th in OKC. Win vs Denver 127-103.

Oklahoma City had all eleven of their top players available for this contest, but it was a close game for the first 3 quarters. OKC was winning 94-91 with 9:18 left when the game turned in OKC's favor. J-Dub made two free throws, followed by Wiggins stealing the ball from Westbrook and releasing Chet for a breakaway dunk. The Nuggets coach got a technical, which gave OKC another point off a free throw. Chet then blocked a layup attempt from Russ. Denver got the loose ball, and Cason blocked a layup from Nnaji. Denver again got the loose ball, and Russ missed a 3-pointer. J-Dub then drained a jump shot. Just 1:19 had passed, and the Thunder lead was now 10 points, and the game was over.

Aaron Gordon only played 7 minutes, while Jamal Murray shot just 6-for-17. The Thunder blocked 14 of Denver's shots, and Russ shot 1-for-9 for just 4 points in 31 minutes. Jokic had 24 points, 13 rebounds, and 9 assists, and Gil Goose added another monster game with 40 points, 8 rebounds, and 3 blocked shots. It was Goose's 3rd straight game with at least 40 points, and all three games were Thunder wins.

March 10th in OKC. Loss vs Denver 127-140.

The Nuggets avenged their loss to the Thunder on the very next day, shooting 60% from the field and making 56% of their 3's. The Thunder gave up the most points in a game that they would all season. The game was close until the 4th quarter started, but the Nuggets went on a 7-16 run to push their 99-101 lead up to 11 points. The Thunder never pulled back into it.

J-Dub only played 14 minutes before doing the splits on a hard fall with Peyton Watson landing on him. He strained his hip on the awful-looking fall. Two of the only games the Thunder had lost this season were the games that Chet and J-Dub were hurt in. Was witnessing those injuries too jarring for our young team to handle in the moment?

This was also the game that Coach Daigneault tried to use Dillon Jones as a permanent sub in an effort to stop Jokic from quickly inbounding the ball. Amongst the many skills Jokic did so well, he was very sneaky at quickly launching the ball all the way down the court on inbounds passes. Coach Daigneault tried to make the refs pause the game at every stoppage to let Jones check in, but Coach Daigneault would then turn down the substitution. The refs didn't put up with it for long, but it showed how visionary and detail-oriented Coach Daigneault was.

Jokic had 35 points, 18 rebounds, and 8 assists for Denver. Lu Dort hit 8 3-pointers in the game to lead OKC with 26 points.

Lu Dort

Lugenz Dort was an absolute Oklahoma City Thunder legend. He was a bowling ball of solid muscle who went undrafted because he couldn't shoot straight. Sam Presti saw his potential, and he convinced Dort to sign a 2-way deal with OKC in the summer of 2019.

Dort's career started off slowly. The Thunder had good players in front of him like Chris Paul, Dennis Schroder, and a young Gil Goose. Turd Ferguson was entrenched at Dort's shooting guard position as the team's defensive stopper. And OKC was pretty good in 2020, so Dort didn't get any play time until the 21st game of the season. Billy Donovan then played him in five straight games, but didn't use him in the next five games after that. Dort played the following two games, then he sat out of ten in a row. But on Game 44 of the 2020 season, Lu Dort entered the starting lineup for good. Then Covid shut the season down.

In the summer of 2020, during the Covid lockdown, Lu Dort's developmental contract was upgraded to a 4-year/ $5.4 million deal, which may be the best contract value ever. When the season resumed in the "Bubble" in Orlando, Dort was entrenched as a starter. He played the first 8 games in Florida, but then hurt his knee, missing the last regular season game and Game 1 of the playoffs.

The Thunder were matched up against the Houston Rockets, and in Game 1 without Dort, James Harden scored 37 points on 12-of-22 shooting. With Dort in the lineup over the next six games, Harden was shut down. The undrafted rookie hounded that year's NBA scoring champion into making just 43-of-105 shots with 16 turnovers. In Game 7, a game that Houston barely won, Harden was Dorted into a 4-for-15 shooting night. The Legend of Lu Dort was born!

I left out Game 5 in the statistics above- James Harden shot 11-of-15 for 31 points that day. But Dort only played 23 minutes in Game 5, because he went 0-for-9 on the wide-open 3-pointers that Houston was daring him to shoot. Dort's poor shooting was a huge issue for him. He shot under 30% from 3 that year, and most of those shots weren't even contested.

Dort's shooting problems weren't just from deep, either- he also shot under 40% from all his field goal attempts. Dort's drives to the hoop seemed to usually end with him blasting the ball off of the backboard hard enough to miss the rim completely. I used to joke that he thought it counted as 2 points if he just hit anything. When I described Gil Goose as silky smooth around the basket, able to finish any shot with either hand, well, early Lu Dort was the opposite of that. But what defense! Dort played so hard, all the time.

Lu Dort had been widely considered one of the NBA's best defenders since his coming out party in the 2020 playoffs. He would only make his first All-NBA Defensive team at the end of the 2025 season, despite being deserving of the honor for years. And his shooting had changed completely, improving from a huge liability to a huge asset. Dort shot his hilarious, sky-ball 3-pointers at an elite 39% in 2024, and finished 2025 at an even better 41%. His finishing at the rim also had become deadly.

Presti gave Dort a new 5-year/$87.5 million contract in the summer of 2022. That contract averaged $17.7 million per year. What was Dort worth in today's NBA? Dort was a 26-year-old 1st team All-NBA defender who shot 41% from 3, and he was a total team player. For comparison:

Player A: 28-year-old wing player, an elite defender with one All-NBA defensive 1st team, 37% career shooter from 3.

Player B: 26-year-old wing player not known for his defense, 41% career shooter from 3.

Player A was Mikel Bridges, a player the Knicks traded four 1st round picks and a 1st round pick swap to get in 2024. Bridges just signed a contract extension for 4-years/ $150 million ($37.5 million per year).

Player B was Desmond Bane, a player that Orlando gave four 1st round picks and a 1st round pick swap to trade for in 2025. His most recent contract was 5-years/ $197 million ($39.5 million per year).

Lu Dort was better than both of those players. He was way underpaid, and he was worth a heck of a lot to other NBA teams. To us fans in Oklahoma, he was invaluable and also beloved. Those boos you heard? That's just us screaming "Luuuuuu!"

March 12th in Boston. Win vs Celtics 118-112.

The Celtics had won 15 of their previous 18 games, so this was a great win away from home by the Thunder. The Celtics attempted 63 (!) 3-pointers. The game was close the whole way. With the teams tied in the 4th quarter 98-98, Boston missed six straight 3-point attempts, while OKC went on an 8-0 run to win.

The Thunder were missing Caruso and J-Dub, while Wiggins missed all 9 of his shots and didn't score. However, seven Oklahoma City players scored in double-figures. Jason Tatum had 33 points, 8 rebounds, and 8 assists, but Jaylen Brown shot 5-of-15 for just 10 points.

March 15th in Detroit. Win vs Pistons 113-107.

The Thunder held on to win this close game, and the Pistons head coach cried during his post-game press conference because the refs were meanies. The Thunder were up by 1 point at halftime, but pulled away in the 3rd quarter, helped by the Pistons melting down. Cade Cunningham got himself ejected in the middle of Detroit receiving four technicals in quick succession. This put the OKC lead up to 88-73.

But the technical fouls lit a fire in the Pistons, and they went on a 24-10 run to make the score 98-97 with 4:16 left. The Thunder were still up 109-105 with just 59 seconds left, but OKC turned the ball over for a five-second violation, giving the Pistons a chance. Hartenstein then blocked an Ausar Thompson layup attempt, leading to an Isaiah Joe 3-point attempt, which missed. However, Kenrich Williams fought for the offensive rebound, and Isaiah Joe got the ball for another 3-pointer, but he missed again. Kenrich got another offensive rebound, and he passed the ball to Hartenstein for a dunk with 23 seconds left to win the game.

Dort got hurt in the game, and the Thunder also played without Chet, J-Dub, and Wiggins, so Kenrich started. Missing so many starters, the

Thunder was forced to end the game with a lineup of Goose, Kenrich, Joe, Hartenstein, and Cason. And those Thunder subs had stepped up to make the big plays to secure the win. Hartenstein had 12 points, 10 rebounds, 3 blocks, and 2 steals, and Gil Goose had an immaculate game of 48 points, making 17 of his 26 shots.

March 16 in Milwaukee. Win vs Bucks 121-105.

The Thunder were winning 46-41 in the 2nd quarter, and then went on a 13-0 run to extend into a big lead. The score was never within single digits again. Lu Dort and J-Dub both missed with injury, so Kenrich started again. Johnny Boy had 21 points, 12 rebounds, and 10 assists, but the Bucks were held to under 40% shooting as a team. Hartenstein had a career-high 24 points to go with 12 rebounds.

March 19th in OKC. Win vs 76ers 133-100.

This was a game that Oklahoma City wanted to lose. Years previous, the 76ers had wanted to get rid of Al Horford and his contract. They salary-dumped him to OKC with a 2025 top-6 protected 1st round pick. Philadelphia's 2025 team had NBA title-winning talent, but injuries had decimated their chances. At the time of this game, the 76ers had the 6th worst record in the NBA. If they could win a few more games in 2025 and stay out of the bottom six picks, the Thunder could end up with their lottery pick in the loaded 2025 draft. The 76ers would most likely recover in 2026, so their 1st round pick that year probably wouldn't be a very good one for the Thunder. And OKC was already going to be the 1-seed in the playoffs anyway. They gave the night off to J-Dub, Dort, Goose, Cason, Caruso, and Hartenstein.

It turned out that Philadelphia had spent years perfecting the art of tanking. Their former GM Sam Hinkie had actually invented the strategy. Their only motivation was to keep their valuable 1st rounder at the end of the season. So, the 76ers still were blown out, despite the Thunder resting so many players. I gambled on the NBA on DraftKings every day, and even I didn't know half of the players that Philadelphia played in the game. Brandon Carlsen got 16 points for the Thunder, while Dillon Jones started and played 36 minutes. The game was over as soon as it started.

The Thunder shot 46% from 3, and the offense was run by Jaylin Williams from the top of the key. J-Will again responded to this opportunity with a triple-double of 19 points, 17 rebounds, and 11 assists. He led the Thunder to victory by dominating Philadelphia with the back-ups to the Oklahoma City back-ups.

Jaylin Williams

Jaylin Williams had been named the Gatorade Player of the Year in Arkansas in high school, and he went to the University of Arkansas where he (unsurprisingly) led the NCAA in charges drawn during his sophomore year. J-Will declared for the draft, and the Thunder picked him in the 2nd round with the 34th pick in 2022.

At 6'8", J-Will was not very tall for a center, but he was big and he didn't get pushed around. He didn't protect above the rim, but was extremely good at drawing charges. He wasn't very athletic, either, but he was very good at stretching a defense with his 39% career 3-point percentage. J-Will was also very outgoing and happy, and seemed to be an important part of the Thunder locker-room.

J-Will started 36 games at center as a rookie, but the Thunder had added Chet and then Hartenstein to the position ahead of him. With J-Will's injury this season he slid down the rotation to probably the 12th best player on the team. But he was a solid player when called upon. And when he was given the minutes and the green light, like in this 76ers game, he crushed it. J-Will had the vision to help a successful NBA offense. I'm not sure he will be in Presti's long term plans, but he was definitely an NBA quality player.

March 21st in OKC. Win vs Charlotte 141-106.

I was invited down to Oklahoma City for this game against a horrible Hornets team with 18 wins and 51 losses. The Thunder jumped out to a 34-14 lead in the 1st quarter. Gil Goose made shot after shot, getting to any spot he wanted. He drained everything, finishing 13-of-18. The Thunder outscored the Hornets 64-26 in the paint by constantly getting to the hoop for easy shots. OKC was deadly from deep, too, making 54% of their 3-pointers. And they were missing J-Dub and Dort, while Goose didn't play at all in the 4th quarter.

Despite all this, the Hornets got the lead down to 75-65 in the 3rd quarter. Charlotte then went 1-for-5 with two shots blocked and a stolen ball, while OKC went on a 20-3 run to put the game away. Oklahoma City clinched the 1-seed in the Western Conference with the win.

70 Game Summary

The Thunder now had 58 wins and 12 losses on the season. The last ten games had included 7 playoff teams, and J-Dub had missed six of the games, while Dort had missed four of them. Additionally, OKC had rested all their best players in two of the games. And the Thunder still won 9 of the 10 games, with Gil Goose recording scoring nights of 51, 48, 41, and 40 points. Nobody wanted to face Oklahoma City.

The Thunder were about to crush the OKC team record of 60 wins in a season. The 1996 Chicago Bulls were historic as the first team to win 70 games.

Could the Thunder win out and get to 70-win immortality? Twelve games to go…

March 23rd in LA. Win vs Clippers 103-101.

Both teams were on 5-game winning streaks, and the Clippers were fighting for their playoff position. OKC, with Chet and J-Dub out, got Lu Dort back, and he forced James Harden into a 4-of-14 shooting night with 6 turnovers. Gil Goose had a tough shooting night as well, going 7-of-29 for 26 points and 8 assists.

The teams stayed within 3 points of each other for the last 8:38 of the extremely tight game. OKC was winning 92-91 with 6:16 left. They then missed three straight 3-pointers and got a shot blocked, but LA was only able to take a small lead at 92-95. The Thunder were winning again, 101-100, with a minute left. OKC's defense forced Norm Powell into a turnover, but Zubac blocked Hartenstein's subsequent layup attempt. Powell then missed a 3-pointer for LA, but Zubac retrieved the offensive rebound. Kawhi had the ball for a final chance as the clock ran down, but he forced up a wayward jump shot after he was double-teamed by Caruso and Cason.

There still wasn't any news on J-Dub's leg injury or prognosis. How hurt was he? The playoffs were getting close.

March 25 in Sacramento. Win vs Kings 121-105.

Oklahoma City shot 59% from 3, outscored Sacramento 42-20 in the paint, and outrebounded the Kings 52-36. The Thunder had a 64-42 lead at the break. But the Kings made a 16-0 run in the 3rd, with Keegan Murray hitting 3 of his 9 3-pointers. This brought the game back within 7 points. However, the Thunder pulled away again in the 4th quarter. J-Dub missed the game again, along with Cason and Wiggins. The Thunder held DeRozan to just 10 points, while Sabonis only scored 8.

March 27th in OKC. Win vs Memphis 125-104.

The Grizzlies' season had nose-dived. They were fighting for their playoff lives after spending a long stretch of the year in 2nd place in the West. Memphis was missing Ja Morant, but Scottie Pippen scored 17 points with 10 rebounds, 7 assists, and 5 steals in his place. JJJ added 27 points, and Memphis kept the game close until the 4th quarter. J-Dub finally returned for OKC after missing 7 games, and he scored 20 points. Gil Goose had a great game of 37 points on 15-of-25 shooting.

Memphis had the score tied at 99 with 7:20 left. The Thunder then went on a 15-0 run, with Memphis going 0-4 with 2 turnovers, a stolen ball, and a shot blocked. Memphis couldn't get back into the game afterward. This was the end of the road for their long-time coach Taylor Jenkins, who was fired the next day.

March 29th in OKC. Win vs Indiana 132-111.

The Pacers were heating up on their way to the Finals, winning 6 of their previous 7 games. After a terrible start to the season, their record was up to 43-30. Oklahoma City was too good, though. They led by 12 points at halftime, and held a double-digit lead over Indiana for the entire second half.

Gil Goose had 33 points, 7 rebounds, and 8 assists. OKC shot 47% from 3, with Lu Dort hitting 6-of-7 3-pointers for 22 points. Chet, J-Will, and Wiggins all missed the game. Hartenstein only played 14 minutes after injuring his hip. Despite missing their big men, OKC still outscored Indiana in the paint 58-40.

March 31st in OKC. Win vs Chicago 145-117.

Chicago had started the season with delusional hopes of winning basketball. But the Bulls were a bad team yet again. Billy Donovan had abandoned Oklahoma City because he didn't want to coach a rebuilding team. Instead, he attached himself to whatever unsuccessful strategy Chicago had deployed for the past six years. I found this hilarious. The Thunder used a 36-13 run in the 2nd quarter to go up 74-40 at halftime, and Isaiah Joe made 8 3-pointers for 31 points.

Oklahoma City had 11 steals while shooting 54% from 3 in this blowout win. Gil Goose scored 27 points with 12 assists in less than 27 minutes. The Thunder had now won 10 games in a row.

April 2nd in OKC. Win vs Detroit 119-103.

The Pistons were jockeying for their playoff seeding in the East, and they fought hard in this game. OKC jumped out to a 41-27 lead in the 1st quarter, but the Pistons narrowed the lead to 65-59 at halftime. The Thunder started the 2nd half with a 10-0 run, and they got their lead back up to 16 at the end of the 3rd quarter. However, Detroit brought it back within 4 points with 6:25 left. The Thunder defense dominated from there, with the Pistons shooting just 2-of-7 with 3 shots blocked, 1 steal, and 3 turnovers to finish.

The Thunder ended up with 12 steals and 19 turnovers forced, and Gil Goose scored 33 points. OKC was missing Wiggins, Caruso, and J-Will, while Detroit was without Cade Cunningham. Chet had 22 points, 11 rebounds, and 6 blocks.

Chet Holmgren

I liked to call Chet our "Baby Giraffe" because he was so tall and so skinny, but also because he looked at times like he was still learning to walk. When he fell on the court it was limbs in all directions, flailing arms and legs, like Bambi on ice.

Chet's value was hard to pinpoint, because he had only played in 114 of 246 regular season games. He missed his entire first season because he dared to jump up into the air and then land back onto the ground. This action caused his foot to shatter. Chet then successfully played his entire "rookie" season in 2024, but he missed over half of the games in 2025 after breaking his hip on a hard, awkward fall.

Holmgren had a massive pedigree, winning National Basketball Player of the Year in high school. He then received 2nd team All-American honors in his one year at Gonzaga. He was drafted with the 2nd pick in the NBA draft, and had been strongly considered for the first pick. Chet then finished second in Rookie of the Year voting in 2024. Holmgren had experienced a lot of amateur success in his past few years.

Holmgren was an outstanding shot blocker, averaging 2.3 blocks per game for his career. He was a great help defender, always looking to meet any penetrating dribbler at the rim. OKC's defense with him had been fantastic.

He was also an elite stretch shooter. Holmgren made over 37% of his 3's on a high volume of over 4 attempts per game, and he stood 7'2". His range allowed OKC to play Hartenstein and Holmgren together without the offense grinding down. OKC also could open the court with five legitimate 3-point shooters by playing Chet at center.

However, Chet was not an offensive juggernaut. He had averaged 16 points a game in his first two years, and he couldn't really create his own shots. He sometimes awkwardly dribbled into a shot, but his out-of-control dribbling was typically something to avoid. It was hilarious to watch, though.

Chet also was not very good at defending opponents one-on-one in the post because he was so skinny. For the same reason, he was not good at gathering rebounds. Chet got pushed around underneath the basket because everyone outweighed him. The 2024 Thunder team's fatal flaw was its lack of rebounding, and Chet was badly exposed by Dallas in the playoffs.

How good of a player will Chet become? He was still really young, and he had missed so much time. I didn't consider him to be part of a "Big 3" on the Thunder. I didn't think he was nearly as good as SGA and Jalen Williams were. I didn't see Chet becoming a candidate for MVP like them. He definitely had the talent to be a multiple time All-Star, though. And he just might make me eat this page in embarrassment. But he didn't yet contribute the production of an elite NBA player. His 15 points per game average in 2025 was 63rd best in the NBA, between Kelly Oubre and Kyle Kuzma. But he did fit perfectly into the Thunder offense in a way that made the sum greater than its parts.

Holmgren played 23 games after returning from his broken hip in 2025, but he did not play very well. He averaged 13.7 points and 7.6 rebounds, and under 2 blocks per game. But he still was extremely valuable as a rim protector and stretch shooter.

But how good could he be? Look at the 8 games he played in the beginning of the season before getting injured (I'm leaving out the game against Portland. Chet only played 18 minutes because the game was a blowout and he was in foul trouble). Holmgren started the season on fire, averaging 20 points and 10 rebounds, with 2.9 blocks per game, while shooting over 40% from 3 in those 8 games. That's who I expect Chet to be in 2026. That Chet Holmgren would be an All-Star player. And if he can be even better than that, look out.

April 4th in Houston. Loss vs Rockets 114-125.

The Thunder had to win their final 6 games to get to 70-win immortality, but any other motivation for them was over until the playoffs started. Meanwhile, Houston was in a dogfight with the Lakers for the 2-seed in the West. This game was never close. The Rockets led 53-69 at halftime, as Sengun scored 31 points and Jalen Freaking Green scored 34. The Thunder brought the score within 9 points with 7:30 left, but Houston went on a 7-2 run, and the score wasn't close again.

Jeff didn't like to see OKC lose. He texted us, "Adams killed us. Chet looked lost out there." Brad replied, "Sloppy turnovers leading to easy buckets. That's usually what the Thunder do to the other team."

April 6th in OKC. Loss vs LA Lakers 99-126.

The Lakers blew OKC out in Oklahoma City, with a 56-78 lead at halftime. As Brad texted during the game, "The Lakers just can't miss a shot right now." Luka the Fat had 30 points, 7 rebounds, and 6 assists, and the Lakers shot 22-of-40 from 3.

The Thunder now had suffered 2 bad losses in a row, as they hadn't been in either game versus the Rockets or the Lakers. This competitive Thunder team didn't suffer bad losses. They barely ever lost at all, and they were usually in most of those losses with a chance to win. Of course, this was the very end of the year, and the games didn't really matter for OKC. But it was concerning.

Besides these last two games, the Thunder had four other "bad" losses this year. The NBA Cup final blowout loss to Milwaukee was the most disappointing game of the season (and that game wasn't an official part of the regular season). The Thunder also got soundly beaten by the Wolves in the game before the All-Star break. Golden State whooped Oklahoma City in November in the same game that Chet broke his hip in. And the Wolves beat Oklahoma City again in February in overtime after OKC had a 25-point lead in the 2nd half.

In 83 games, Oklahoma City only had 6 games that were disappointing. And four of those losses were kind of understandable, even if the effort and execution were lacking (the Chet murder, the All-Star week early vacation, and these two end of the season games).

Only the Wolves inexplicable comeback and the beatdown from Milwaukee with a title on the line were truly disappointing. And in the other 77 games this season, the Thunder passed out an NBA-record 54 wins by 10 points or more. The consistent excellence that Oklahoma City displayed didn't happen often in the NBA. Only a handful of all-time great teams had been able to put together a season like the 2025 Thunder.

April 8th in OKC. Win vs LA Lakers 136-120.

After conceding two straight losses for only the second time this season, the Thunder returned to winning. The Lakers were up 97-98 as the 4th quarter started, but the game turned to OKC's favor when Luka the Fat was ejected for trash-talking an Oklahoma City fan. Luka had made a jump shot to put the Lakers up by a point with 7:40 to go, and he let a spectator in the stands know about it. But a sensitive ref thought that Doncic was speaking to him. Luka tried to plead his case, but after spending his entire career constantly whining to the refs about calls he didn't like, the refs had tuned him out. OKC went on a 29-12 run afterward to win the game.

The Thunder were 18-for-37 from 3, while the Lakers were 18-for-40. As Jay texted during the game, "3-point competition tonight. This game is awesome. Neither team can miss." Gil Goose scored 42 points. The Thunder outscored the Lakers 56-32 in the paint, while the Lakers turned the ball over 19 times.

April 9th in Phoenix. Win vs Suns 125-112.

The Suns had started the season 8-1 to make people think they were good. They finished poorly from there, with a 28-45 record. While they were still in contention for a playoff spot at the end of the season, Phoenix had lost 7 straight games. They were a toxic team.

Oklahoma City rested Goose, Hartenstein, Dort, and Cason. The Thunder were down by 5 points at halftime, but OKC outscored Phoenix 43-26 in the 3rd quarter to take the lead. Kevin Durant didn't play, and some guy I'd never heard of named Gillespie scored 17 points in 23 minutes for the Suns.

This was also the game that J-Dub tore a ligament in his shooting hand. He injured himself fighting for a steal with Devin Booker at the beginning of the second half. J-Dub would play hurt throughout the playoffs, and he had to have surgery on his hand in the offseason.

April 11th in Salt Lake City. Win vs Jazz 145-111.

Oklahoma City was up by 15 points at halftime, and they won every quarter in a game that was never in doubt. The Thunder rested Goose, J-Dub, Hartenstein, Chet, Dort, and Cason, so J-Will was put in charge of the team's offense for the 3rd time this season. He responded with a third win and his third triple-double in those situations. J-Will finished with 15 points, 11 rebounds, and 10 assists, while Aaron Wiggins scored 35 points. Isaiah Joe hit 10 3-pointers on his way to 32 points.

The Jazz had lost 19 of their last 21 games in yet another miserable season. Sensabaugh scored 25 points, Filipowski had 15 points and 13 rebounds, and Mykhailiuk had 27 points- who are these guys? A big surprise was the return of Ajay Mitchell! He had been out of action since January 3rd after surgery on his toe.

April 13th in NOLA. Win vs Pelicans 115-100.

OKC led 38-19 after the 1st quarter, and the stand-in Pelicans could never get back in the game.

They faced Oklahoma City with players such as Lester Quinones (34 minutes), Antonio Reeves (39 minutes), and Keion Brooks (39 minutes). I didn't know who any of those players were.

Oklahoma City again rested Goose, J-Dub, Hartenstein, Chet, Dort, and Cason. J-Will couldn't shine in their place, because he hurt his ankle after 2 minutes. Aaron Wiggins finished with 28 points, 7 rebounds, and 7 assists, and Brendan Carlson had 26 points, 10 rebounds, and 3 blocks. Kenrich provided 17 points and 12 rebounds, and Dillon Jones added 13 points and 10 rebounds.

82 Game Summary

The Thunder started their final 12 games by playing 9 straight games against teams fighting for their playoff positions. OKC won 7 of those 9 games. The Thunder then finished the season against 3 terrible teams, and crushed all 3 teams despite resting their best players.

Oklahoma City finished the 2025 season with an outstanding 68 wins! The team had set all kinds of NBA records. They had tried to lose games, but won anyways. They had rested all their best players, but still won. The Thunder were clearly the best team in the NBA. But their regular season accomplishments didn't matter anymore after the playoffs began.

The only thing left for OKC was waiting to find out who they would face in the first round: Golden State, Memphis, Dallas, or Sacramento.

The Playoffs

NBA Playoffs Round 1

The Grizzlies had shown a lot of promise during the season before completely collapsing. Memphis was 18-8 and in 2nd place in the West in mid-December. They were 32-16 and still in 2nd place at the beginning of February. At the beginning of March they were slumping, but were just one game out of 2nd place. On March 28th, with just 9 games left before the playoffs started, they fired their head coach. They struggled to a 10 win and 12 loss finish, leaving them in 8th place, and consigning them to the Play-In round. After losing to Golden State for the chance to play the 2-seed Houston, they regrouped to win one last time versus Dallas. This gave them the opportunity to get swept out of the playoffs by the Thunder.

Memphis had other troubles, too. Jaylen Wells, their frontrunner for Rookie of the Year, suffered a broken wrist in April. The injury ended his season. And their star player Ja Morant endured multiple injuries that limited him to just 50 games. Ja also caused national controversy on April 1st by pretending his fingers were pistols. The league office informed him that he was no longer allowed to pretend his fingers were pistols, because that's from a child's game called Cops and Robbers. Furthermore, any recurrence of this horrific gesture would earn him a fine equivalent to an average

American's annual salary. In response, Ja Morant repeated the motion the very next day.

The Grizzlies had created another problem for themselves as well. Their new coach expected the team to change into a more sharing and passing offense. But their two star players Ja and JJJ liked isolation plays and pick-and-rolls. They were not happy about the changes being forced upon them. Not happy at all.

Most miserable in this disaster of a season, I could only imagine, were the fans of the Memphis Grizzlies. A quick recap of their last four years… in the 2022 season this was a super-young, super-deep team. Their 3 most important players were Ja Morant (22 years-old), Desmond Bane (23 years-old), and Jaren Jackson Jr (22 years-old). Steven Adams was the team veteran, and he was just 28 years-old. Morant was only in his third season, yet he made it onto the All-NBA 2nd team (Gil Goose made his first All-NBA team in his fifth season). The Grizzlies finished with 56 wins, and they were the 2-seed in the Western Conference (the Thunder finished that same season in 14th place).

Memphis followed up that promising season with 51 wins and another 2nd place finish in 2023. The Grizzlies were loaded with talent, they were very young, and they were winning games. Expectations were sky-high for the years ahead.

Instead, they self-destructed. The previous year they had let Kyle Anderson leave in free agency and had traded DeAnthony Melton, losing two important bench players. Then, the Memphis GM decided that he had to jettison Dillon Brooks. He was their defensive enforcer who had just made the 2023 All-Defense 2nd team. But Brooks had antagonized LeBron in the 2023 playoffs. Brooks' taunts were blamed for motivating LeBron to end Memphis' season.

Dillon Brooks was given away to Houston for basically nothing. To replace him, Memphis traded for Marcus Smart, a player who formerly was very good at defense. Also acquired with Marcus Smart was Marcus Smart's very big contract. All Memphis had to give up in the trade was two first round picks and their backup point guard Tyus Jones.

Dillon Brooks joined a Houston team that only won 22 games in 2023. He helped push them to 41 wins in 2024, and then 52 wins in 2025. Meanwhile, Marcus Smart played just 39 lackluster games for Memphis over a season-and-a-half. Memphis then traded him away. Memphis' GM had to attach another 1st round pick to the trade just to move Smart's contract off the roster.

But their situation got even worse. Before the 2024 season, Ja Morant was suspended for 25 games because he liked to make parody videos of 1990's rap songs. He returned after his suspension for only 9 games before he tore his shoulder. The injury ended his season (it would have been quite useful for Memphis to have their backup point guard Tyus Jones during this time).

The 2024 Memphis Grizzlies finished in 13th place in the West with just 27 wins. In response to the General Manager's malfeasance in overseeing this debacle, the General Manager fired all of the assistant coaches. Instead of firing the head coach as well, the GM hired his future head coach. And the GM told the head coach that the future head coach was the head coach's new assistant coach.

Things moved fast in the NBA. It was important to remember that Memphis was the "Can't Miss" team of the NBA just two years ago, not the Thunder. It was quite a sad situation for the Memphis Grizzlies. I would feel bad for them if I didn't hate the Memphis Grizzlies.

Memphis used to be our huge rivals. Durant, Russ, and Ibaka vs Zac Randolph, Mike Conley, Marc Gasol, and Tony Allen. Grind City.

2011 playoffs

Western Conference Semifinals, OKC wins in 7 games (Game 4 went to Triple Overtime!).

2013 playoffs

Western Conference Semifinals, Memphis wins in 5 games versus the best Thunder team of the Durant era (OKC had been decimated when Westbrook was murdered by Pat Beverly, though).

2014 playoffs

1st round, Oklahoma City wins in 7 games (an unprecedented 4 straight games went to Overtime!).

Oklahoma City and Memphis spent years battling against each other in epic playoff series. Let the postseason begin!

Game 1 in OKC. Win vs Memphis 131-80.

The largest margin of victory in NBA playoff history was 58 points. The Thunder just missed that record while winning this game. OKC was up 32-20 at the end of the 1st quarter. Just four minutes later the score was 51-22. Memphis' turnovers had led to dagger 3's and fast break dunks by Cason, J-Dub, and Hartenstein during a 20-0 run. The halftime score was 68-36, and the game was over.

The Thunder generated 12 steals, 8 blocks, and 24 turnovers in the game. Memphis' best 3 players (Morant, JJJ, and Bane) finished a combined 11-of-42 for 30 points. Marvin Bagley came off the bench to score 17 points in 16 minutes. This gave OKC another advantage, as he would probably get more playing time in the games ahead.

15 wins to go.

Game 2 in OKC. Win vs Grizzlies 118-99.

The Thunder jumped out to a 32-17 lead in the 1st quarter, as Memphis missed its first ten shots. The Thunder repeatedly got wide open 3-point opportunities and easy drives to the basket. With 2:05 left in the 2nd quarter and OKC leading 63-43, Alex Caruso missed a 3-pointer. The ball caromed long to start a fast break for Memphis. Somehow, Isaiah Joe outran two Memphis players to the ball. He turned around and set himself to nail a 3-pointer. I thought the game was over right there.

However, the Thunder missed all their 3-point attempts in the 3rd quarter, and their lead was whittled down to 11 points. Then Alex Caruso took over in the 4th quarter. He started by making a 3-pointer, then threw an assist to Cason for a dunk. He followed that by blocking a Ja Morant shot in the paint, and hit a turnaround jumper. Memphis' first five possessions resulted in two missed shots, two blocked shots, and a turnover. The Thunder lead had grown to 99-79 in under 3 minutes. Memphis wouldn't come back, and OKC took a 2-0 series lead.

Gil Goose was only 10-of-29 in the game for 27 points, but Chet had 20 points, 11 rebounds, and 5 blocks. Ja Morant was Dorted again with a 10-of-25 game. His sidekicks played much better, as Desmond Bane had 19 points and 12 rebounds, and JJJ had 26 points. Marvin Bagley unsurprisingly had 0 points and 2 turnovers. The Thunder had 8 blocks and 8 steals, and OKC outrebounded Memphis 55 to 42.

14 wins to go.

Game 3 in Memphis. Win vs Grizzlies 114-108.

This was a tale of two halves. Memphis came out at home and crushed Oklahoma City from the start, only for the Thunder to launch a second half comeback for the ages. The first half was full of excitement for Memphis, both good but also bad. Memphis made 11 of their 22 3-point attempts in the opening 24 minutes, with Scottie Pippen going 5-for-6. As Brad texted us while it was happening, "This may be the game the Thunder lose because Memphis shoots 50% from 3." Memphis scored 77 first half points, which must be the most points the Thunder defense gave up in the first half all season (Not true. OKC let the Lakers score 78 first half points in April. OKC also gave up 77 first half points to San Antonio in March). OKC also was ice cold on 3's in the first half at 22%.

A typical sequence happened with 5 minutes left in the half. Pippen dribbled from midcourt right by Goose and all the way to the rim, with no resistance, for an easy layup. Goose went the other way and tried to dribble into the lane, but Pippen stole the ball. Pippen then released Morant for a breakaway dunk. The crowd was going crazy. Jeff texted what we were all feeling. "Well, this sucks."

However, the whole series changed with 3:15 to go before halftime. The Grizzlies were winning by 27 points. Pippen stole the ball from the Thunder and he started a fast break. He went up for a layup with Dort defending from behind, so Pippen dropped a pass to a trailing Morant. Morant went up for one of his signature monster jams, but Dort hadn't bitten on Pippen's fake shot. As Dort turned to defend Morant, his feet slipped out from under him. He undercut Morant, who fell hard onto his hip. Ja was seriously injured, and he had to be scraped off the court and helped to the locker room. Morant was done for the game and for the series. Jay said he had hurt himself because, "Ja Morant landed on his Glock pistol."

If the Thunder lost this road playoff game, the setback would not be unsurmountable. My brother thought the game was over, and he went to bed. Brad wasn't happy. He texted us, "Miss a 3 or turn it over on offense is a good way of getting down by 30. Looks like Game 5 coming back home." But I believed this Thunder team was too good not to mount a comeback.

The Thunder started burying 3-pointers, and OKC just crushed Memphis in the 3rd quarter. The Grizzlies shot 5-of-16, and scored only 18 points while turning the ball over 7 times. Chet hit 4 3-pointers and scored 16 points by himself. When J-Dub hit a 3-pointer at the buzzer to end the 3rd, Memphis' 26-point halftime lead was already down to only 8 points.

The Thunder did not let up in the 4th quarter. A Chet dunk with 9:18 left put the Thunder down by 6. With 8:42 left, Goose stepped back into a 3, and sunk it. The Thunder were down by 3. The Thunder tied the game with 5 minutes left at 105-105. Memphis took the lead back, but a Chet 3-pointer tied the game again with 2:38 left. A J-Dub free throw put OKC up by 1 point with 1:20 remaining. But Memphis had the ball. The Grizzlies were able to get Desmond Bane free for a good look from 3, but he missed the shot. Chet was fouled, and he made both free throws for a 3-point lead. On the next play, Pippen tried to dribble at the 3-point line against Caruso. Caruso knocked the ball free and tied it up with 40 seconds left.

OKC won the jump ball, and Dort was fouled. However, he missed both of his free throws. This gave Memphis another chance to tie the game.

They were able to swing it to Jon Konchar in the corner for a wide-open 3, but he missed. OKC secured the rebound with 25 seconds left, and quickly released Caruso for a fast break layup. This put the Thunder up by 5 points and ended the game. OKC had come back from a 29-point deficit to win. It was the biggest playoff comeback win in the NBA since 1997.

Chet scored 23 of his 24 points in the second half to lead the charge. Memphis had only scored 13 points in the 4th quarter with the game on the line. I texted "Caruso in the last five minutes was the best possible basketball defense you could ever hope for. What. A. Player. No way to score on that closing lineup. They could barely get the ball down the court."

13 wins to go.

Game 4 in Memphis. Win vs Grizzlies 117-115.

Memphis was without Ja Morant, victim of an unintentional and unfortunate injury to his leg, so Santi Aldama entered the starting lineup. Scottie Pippen was tasked with running the Grizzlies' offense. He was signed from the Lakers in the summer of 2023 as a 2-way project, but was now one of Memphis' most important players.

I thought the Grizzlies would roll over after losing Ja to injury and then capitulating in Game 3.

Jay also was confident, texting, "1, 2, 3, Cancun!" But Memphis came to play in this one. It was exciting and close throughout, with 8 ties and 15 lead changes. Zach Edey had 7 blocks for the Grizzlies! OKC was also hurt by missing 25 of their first 29 3-point attempts, and by Memphis outrebounding OKC 51-33.

The 4th quarter started 88-85, but the Thunder started to pull away. When Gil Goose stepped back into a 3 with 3:38 left, he gave OKC a 12-point lead. However, Memphis showed their spirit with a 10-0 run to get right back in it. Vince Williams hit a corner 3 with 2:46 left to make it a 7-point game, and Santi Aldama made a corner 3 with 1:52 left to pull within 2 points. J-Dub then ended Memphis' streak with a jump shot, but it was answered by a Pippen drive for a layup. Gil Goose then used a pick to set up for a 3-point shot, which he missed.

Pippen attacked with a chance to tie with 1:09 remaining. He was able to drive all the way to the basket, but he hesitated when Chet slid over to him. Chet took advantage of Pippen's indecision to just steal the ball away. Holmgren was then fouled, and he made both of his free throws for a 112-108 lead. Memphis then set up a 3-point attempt for Desmond Bane, but he missed it. Lu Dort rebounded the ball, and was fouled. The Thunder had a 6-point lead with 49 seconds left after Dort made his free throws. But the Grizzlies still wouldn't die.

Memphis attacked the Thunder defense, then passed around the key to find an open Vince Williams for another 3. 114-111. Gil Goose ran the shot clock down to five, then started his drive against a back-pedaling Williams. Goose spun around and stepped back into a long 2-point attempt, draining it. 116-111. Bane sprinted down to the other end, and he quickly sunk a long 3-pointer with 7 seconds left. 116-114. J-Dub was fouled on the inbounds pass, and he missed one of his free throws. 117-114. Memphis had a chance to tie, but Coach Daigneault had Lu Dort foul Desmond Bane before he could attempt a 3. Bane made his first free throw before purposely missing his 2nd. JJJ tipped the rebound towards the basket for the tie, but it went wide. Memphis' season was over.

JJJ only scored 12 points on 3-of-12 shooting while turning the ball over 5 times. Scottie Pippen was outstanding again with 30 points and 11 rebounds. Gil Goose starred with 38 points, and Hartenstein added 11 points, 12 rebounds, and 4 of OKC's 13 steals.

12 wins to go.

NBA Playoffs Round 2

Meanwhile, the Western Conference playoffs continued for 6 other teams. The teams seeded 3 through 8 barely had any difference between their records in 2025 (Lakers-50 wins, Nuggets-50 wins,

Clippers-50 wins, Wolves-49 wins, Warriors-48 wins, Grizzlies-48 wins). It wasn't a huge upset when Minnesota beat the 3-seed Lakers 4 games to 1. Golden State also took down the 2-seed Houston in 7 games. But the Thunder's next opponent was the Denver Nuggets.

Denver won the NBA title with this team in 2023. Now, they were older and they were hurting. They had just endured a tough 7-game series against the Clippers, and they probably should have been swept by Los Angeles in four games. They now had to travel to OKC with just one day of rest. Oklahoma City had not played for 8 straight days.

Denver had other obstacles, too. Nepo-child Josh Kroenke had fired the Nuggets' long-time head coach Mike Malone just 3 games before the playoffs started. He did this because he didn't like the team's "vibes". Their new interim head coach was the young David Adelman. I found he had a delightful resemblance to Alfred E. Neuman from MAD magazine. Every time the camera panned to him, I'd say "What, me worry?" out loud. Unfortunately, he gave me a lot to worry about in this series.

And that was because.... the Denver Nuggets had a guy. Nikola Jokic was the best basketball player in the world, and he had been single-handedly dragging this team up the mountain for years. With him, Denver would always have a chance to win. He had finished 1st or 2nd in MVP voting for the past five years in a row.

Jokic famously had never had a teammate good enough to be named to an All-Star team or All-NBA team in his entire career. If Jokic had any additional help at all, they could have been a dynasty. He wished he had a sidekick like Jalen Williams. He dreamed of having a bench as good as OKC's. Heck, he dreamed of having a bench at all. But they still were a contending team every year because of him.

The Thunder's Gil Goose deservedly won MVP this season, and what an outstanding player he was. When I called Jokic the best basketball player in the world, I knew my fellow Oklahomans would construe it as a huge insult towards our beloved Gil Goose. But Jokic was a plus at every basketball skillset that there was. He was absolutely unstoppable. He was widely considered the best passing big man in NBA history, and always was near the league leaders in assists. Jokic could shoot 3's. He could make midrange shots. He could post up and brutalize defenders. Jokic did whatever he wanted to on the court. And it was like he could see 5 seconds into the future in the way he anticipated rotations, cutting teammates, and pick-and-rolls. I wouldn't ever trade Goose for Jokic. Nobody would-Jokic was already 30 years-old. But I think if the

Thunder had the choice of SGA or Jokic for the 2026 season, I'd pick Jokic.

*****

The Nuggets basically had 6 players they relied upon for their playoff rotation. Micheal Porter was severely limited with an injured shoulder. And Russ Westbrook couldn't shoot (he would end up shooting 7-of-32 on 3-pointers against Oklahoma City this series). Denver's talent was far inferior to Oklahoma City's.

The Nuggets played zone defense against OKC for large amounts of the series. The Denver zone was really effective because Jokic never left the lane, and the referees never called him for 3-second violations. The Thunder also seemed afraid to drive in on Jokic. He was a good defender, but he wasn't a great rim protector. The Thunder's lack of aggression limited them to jump shots and 3-pointers in their half-court offense.

Game 1 in OKC. Loss vs Nuggets 119-121.

Game 1 was tragic. After the Thunder followed up their outstanding regular season with a sweep of the Grizzlies, the chatter on the internets had been "would the Thunder go 16-0 in the playoffs?" Ridiculous. But I would not have guessed the Nuggets could win this particular game.

Both teams played great basketball at the highest skill level. Gil Goose had a beautiful play just three minutes into the game. He dribbled into lane against Christian Braun, pump-faked him into the air, and then pirouetted 360 degrees around him. This freed Goose to take an uncontested jump shot that he drained from the free throw line. Vintage SGA!

The Thunder were in control all game, but the Nuggets stayed right with them. The NBA's two superstars both showed out, with Goose getting 33 points, 10 rebounds, and 8 assists, and Jokic having a massive 42 points and 22 rebounds. Denver handily outrebounded OKC 43-63, and outscored them in the paint 46-54, but the OKC defense had 12 steals and 11 blocks.

The Thunder had worked their lead at a rocking Paycom Center up to a massive 13 points with just 6:30 to go, and Jokic had picked up 5 fouls. The game was well in hand, and confidence was high. With under two minutes left, and down by 6, Jokic backed Caruso down into the lane, and flipped the ball up and in. With 1:11 left and down by 4, Jokic got the ball on the top of the key. He shot his way behind his head, non-jump shot over Hartenstein and swished it for a 1-point game. With 25 seconds left and still down by 1 point, the Nuggets got the ball to Russ for a 3-pointer, which he missed (of course). But Aaron Gordon got the offensive rebound, and he spun into a layup attempt. J-Dub flew in to stuff him and preserve the Thunder lead. Disaster averted. Gil Goose ended up with the ball, and he was fouled with 14 seconds left.

Goose made both of his free throws to put OKC up by 3 points. Then the Thunder got really bad with their game management. First, they immediately fouled Jokic instead of letting the clock run. Jokic made both free throws to bring Denver within 1 point again. On OKC's inbounds pass, Gil Goose cannily slipped the defense to make a wide-open layup, and it put the Thunder back up by 3 with 11 seconds left.

Denver was out of timeouts, so they couldn't advance the ball to inbound from the frontcourt. The 5 seconds were ticking, and they were frantic. Most importantly, Jokic was on the bench. The Nuggets had not wanted him to foul out when the Thunder had the ball. Denver expected to sub him back in on a Thunder free throw attempt. But when Goose made a field goal instead, it left Jokic stranded for Denver's pivotal last play. Could Denver's offense make a play without Jokic?

The Thunder then did the absolute worst thing possible for the situation. Coach Daigneault wanted OKC to foul Denver before they could try a 3-point attempt for the tie. However, Caruso fouled Aaron Gordon as soon as he caught the inbounds pass in the backcourt. Instead of forcing Denver to dribble up the court and take time off the clock, Caruso had put Gordon at the line immediately. This also let Denver get Jokic back on the court.

Gordon made both free throws. OKC was still up by 1 point. Chet was then fouled with 9 seconds left. He missed both of his free throws with the game on the line. Christian Braun rebounded the 2nd miss for Denver. He launched the ball to Russ on the run. Russ threw a quick cross-court pass to a wide-open Aaron Gordon in the corner for a 3-pointer. Gordon nailed the shot with 3 seconds left to put Denver up by 2 points. J-Dub then missed a shot from his own half as the buzzer sounded. What in the hell just happened?

It was a shocking, shocking loss. Coach Daigneault said in the postgame that his strategy was always to foul when up by 3 points at the end of games. The Thunder had been using that strategy, including in the previous game against Memphis just nine days prior. But the Thunder had used the strategy sparingly. Their opponents rarely had a chance to win at the very end of games, because most of their games weren't close at all.

Daigneault's strategy itself wasn't controversial, and it was mathematically sound. But the clock was the enemy of the team that was losing, and it only made sense to foul after the clock ran down. Any fan of March Madness knew all this. Stopping the clock and giving free throws to the team that was losing was exactly what that team wanted.

I also thought Coach Daigneault might be taking the blame to protect Caruso. The players obviously knew their coach wanted to foul. But to foul that quickly was such a bad play by such a good player. However, they also had fouled Jokic too quickly on the Nugget's previous possession. Maybe Coach Daigneault was to blame, and he needed to adjust his strategy. Jeff texted, "We got outcoached by a guy that's coached for three weeks."

It was such an upsetting game. The stakes were so large, and the expectations were so high. The game was totally in hand, with a 13-point lead in the 4th quarter against an old and tired team on the road. This Thunder team never lost these types of games. It was a total gut punch.

Game 2 in OKC. Win vs Nuggets 149-106.

I went down to Oklahoma City for this game. Walking in Bricktown with my friend Brad, I confessed that I wasn't nervous at all. This OKC team always responded to adversity. The Thunder hadn't lost two straight home games since November 2023. Jeff texted me, "Nuggets are in trouble." I texted him back, "Nuggets are in big, big trouble." I thought it would be a blowout, and I was right. The game was over from the moment it started.

The stadium was so, so loud. We Thunder fans consider ourselves to be an extension of the team, and we wanted to do our part to help them win. If the Thunder had the ball, it was "O-K-C" over and over again, reverberating from the rafters. When Denver had the ball, we yelled "Dee-Fence. Dee-Fence". It was too deafening for us to hear the refs blow the whistle up in Loud City.

The Thunder made 71% of their shots in the 1st quarter, and they more than doubled the Nuggets' score, 45-21. The Thunder then set an NBA playoff record for most points in a 1st half with 87. Jokic purposely fouled out of the game in the 3rd quarter so he could rest. The score was an outstanding 124-76 (!) after three quarters. Gil Goose put on a masterclass performance, with 34 points and 8 assists in just 30 minutes on 11-of-13 shooting. The Thunder had 12 steals and 8 blocks, and drove into the paint to outscore Denver 52-28 down low.

Jokic summed it up in the postgame, saying "Basically it was one team playing tonight." But despite suffering the most embarrassing defeat of his career, he was heading home happy. Denver had stolen a playoff game in Oklahoma City.

11 wins to go.

Game 3 in Denver. Loss vs Nuggets 104-113.

The game was close the entire way, and the teams were tied at 97-97 with under 4 minutes to play. Both teams were beating each other up in this very physical contest, and the referees were letting it all go. J-Dub missed a layup, and there was a scrum for the rebound. J-Dub recovered the ball, and he went up again, only to be hammered by two defenders. Hartenstein tried to get to the rebound, and he was hammered. The Nuggets took the ball down the court, and Jamal Murray tried to dribble by Dort, but he was hand-checked in the chest and stood up. He tried to go at Goose again, but got spun around, then threw up a backwards layup that was blocked by Chet. It was still 97 all with 2:20 left when Murray took on Hartenstein. He dribbled into a long fadeaway shot from the corner, and drained it. Gil Goose then dribbled in on the defense, before kicking it out to J-Dub for a 3-pointer. J-Dub sunk it for a 1-point OKC lead.

The OKC lead was up to 3 points with 30 seconds left, but Jamal Murray had the ball at the top of the key. Four Thunder defenders collapsed onto his pick-and-roll with Jokic. This let Aaron Gordon sneak to the corner unguarded. Murray found Gordon, and he drained his 3-pointer to tie the game with 26 seconds left. Gil Goose then waited until 10 seconds remained to begin his attack on Christian Braun. He started on the left, before dribbling back across the free throw line for an off-balance jump shot. He missed. Denver called timeout to set up a corner 3-pointer for Jokic, which was contested, but makeable. His shot clanged off the rim, and the teams went to overtime.

Denver scored on its first two overtime possessions. Jokic made a basket on a slow, twisting drive, and Micheal Porter followed with a catch-and-shoot 3-pointer. It kept going downhill from there for OKC. The Thunder possessions in overtime ended with: miss, miss, turnover, miss, but offensive rebound, then blocked shot, dunk (!) at 1:56, miss, miss, blocked shot. Denver outscored OKC in overtime 2 to 11.

Chet and Hartenstein both had double-doubles, and OKC outscored Denver 56-32 in the paint. But the Thunder shot 9-for-35 from 3 for the game. Goose was 1-of-6, Chet was 1-of-6, and Dort was 0-of-4. J-Dub had 32 points, but Gil Goose played poorly, shooting 7-of-22. Jokic also played poorly, shooting 8-for-25 with 8 turnovers for 20 points and 16 rebounds, while going 0-for-10 on his 3-point attempts. His teammates picked him up, though. All five Denver starters played at least 42 minutes, and Jamal Murray ended up with 27 points, 8 assists, and 4 steals. Micheal Porter had 21 points and 8 rebounds, and Aaron Gordon had 22 points and 8 rebounds.

It was so depressing. The Thunder's domination in Game 2 was representative of the talent discrepancy between the two teams. Games 1 and 3 should have been Thunder wins, but they somehow became awful losses. The inexperienced OKC players had been flamboozled by the Denver veterans. Denver was somehow in control of the series, up 2 games to 1. Game 4 in Denver was must-win for OKC, and the brilliant Thunder season was already on the brink of being over. The vibes in Oklahoma were not good.

Game 4 in Denver. Win vs Nuggets 92-87.

Game 4 was played on a Sunday afternoon. It was a quick turnaround from Friday night's late overtime game. This game started out great for the Thunder, as they held the Nuggets to just 8 (!) points in the 1st quarter, with Denver going a dismal 2-for-22 with 5 turnovers. Brad texted, "We set an NBA record for lowest point total in a quarter. That's pretty awesome." I tweeted back, "4-for-30 on 3-pointers, with 18 turnovers and 7 airballs." That wasn't true, but that was the way it felt. OKC couldn't shoot either, though, making only 34% of their shots in the 1st half. Brad texted, "Do you enjoy terrible basketball? Because we are watching it." Despite Denver's historically putrid start to the game, the Nuggets had taken a 6-point lead on OKC by the end of the 3rd quarter.

J-Dub was just 2-of-13 for 10 points, and Lu Dort only made 2 of his 10 3-point attempts. Denver kept daring Dort to shoot, and he only played 19 minutes in the game due to his off night. The Thunder were saved by their bench mob of Caruso, Wiggins, and Cason playing big minutes, and those three were 8-of-14 on their 3-pointers.

Jamal Murray shot 5-of-15, and Westbrook missed 7 of his 9 3-point attempts. Aaron Gordon had 15 points and 16 rebounds, but Jokic shot just 7-of-22 for 27 points and 13 rebounds. The Thunder had concentrated on shutting down his passing, and Jokic had just 21 assists with 23 turnovers in the first four games.

The Thunder were winning 84-80 with 3 minutes left, and attacking against the Denver zone defense. The Nuggets were shading their defenders strongly towards Gil Goose, so he switched the ball over to J-Dub, who drove hard to the hoop for a layup.

On the next OKC possession, Goose split the first two zone defenders up top, and drove in for another layup to go up by 7 points with 2:20 left. With 1:30 to go, Aaron Gordon dribbled past Chet, before laying it off to Jokic for an easy lay-in. OKC was up by 5. Goose then lost his dribble with 1:13 to go, but Micheal Porter missed a jump shot on the next possession. Goose missed his next jumper with 30 seconds left, but Jamal Murray missed a quick 3 for Denver. There were 23 seconds left, and OKC still led 88-83, and they had the ball.

Russ fouled J-Dub after the inbounds, and he made both free throws to push the lead to 7 points. Caruso then made another bad end of the game defensive play. He fouled Aaron Gordon on a 3-point attempt with just 8 seconds left. Gordon missed the first shot, made the second one, and then purposely missed his third free throw. The ref blew for a foul before the ball was rebounded, calling lane violations on Chet and Jokic.

This bizarre call resulted in a jump ball, which was deflected to Gordon. He threw up a desperation 3-pointer, and his shot banked in with 2 seconds left to bring Denver back within 3 points. OKC got their inbounds pass to J-Dub, and he was fouled. J-Dub made his free throws to finally end the game.

The misery of this series had continued. Up by 7 points and under 10 seconds left, Oklahoma City almost lost this game. How was this not way easier? OKC was so much better than this bunch of walking zombies from Denver.

I texted, "This whole Thunder season has been so much fun. Until this series. Two terrible losses, one terrible win, and one game just to tease us with how much more talented we are than Denver. Just sucking my soul away." Brad replied, "They keep it close, slow the game down and shoot free throws. Trail the whole game then win late. The Thunder are way better than this team but not as smart. They're causing me to lose sleep, and not because the games end at midnight, but because the dumb way they finish close games."

The Thunder headed back home for another must-win contest in Game 5. Jeff texted, "And yet, we have a great opportunity to win in two days. Think positive, men."

10 wins to go.

Game 5 in OKC. Win vs Nuggets 112-105.

Brad said, "The Thunder need to push the pace and move the ball on this tired 6-man rotation." OKC did just that, and they won, despite Nikola Jokic dominating with 44 points on 17-of-25 shooting with 15 rebounds.

Denver missed 8 of their first 9 shots in the game, but they heated up to lead by 11 points in the 2nd quarter. The Thunder followed with a 9-0 run to end the half. This got the Nuggets' lead down to 2 points, but Denver pushed their lead back up to 8 points heading into the 4th quarter.

Denver was up 81-90 with 8:25 to go, but Lu Dort hit 3 straight 3-pointers to cut the lead to just 2 points. With 4:45 left, Gil Goose had a 3-point attempt to take the lead, but he missed. The ball caromed into the corner, and Dort came flying in at full speed, diving out-of-bounds to save it. J-Dub swung the ball to J-Will. He faked a 3 and drove in, then dropped the ball to Chet for a layup. This amazing hustle play tied the game at 94.

The teams traded baskets for 96-96, then SGA drove in for a spinning layup to take the lead with 3:20 left. Jamal Murray took the next possession and drove in for a layup, but Chet blocked his shot. The ball unfortunately went right to Jokic for a tip-in to tie the score at 98-98. 3:05 to go. Gil Goose took the Thunder ball and drove in. As the defense collapsed on him, Hartenstein was freed to roll to the basket for an alley-oop and a 2-point lead. 2:46 to go. Jokic took the next possession at the top of the key against Hartenstein, drove around him, and laid the ball in high off of the glass to tie it back up at 100-100. 2:22 to go. Gil Goose took the Thunder possession. He hit a step-back jumper from the free throw line, while being fouled. This put the Thunder up by 3 points. 2 minutes left.

The Thunder defense swarmed Denver on their next possession, stunting their offense. With the shot clock winding down, Jokic got the ball at the 3-point line. Chet was all over him, and Jokic pirouetted into a heavily contested 3-point attempt. He somehow swished the shot to tie the game yet again. Magic. 1:40 to go. Gil Goose then drove in on the defense, and passed out to Dort, who swung it to J-Dub wide-open in the corner. J-Dub drained the 3-pointer to put OKC back up by 3. 1:18 to go.

The two teams had kept trading baskets down the stretch, playing immaculate basketball under the highest of pressure. But the Nuggets finally cracked. Micheal Porter missed a 3-point attempt with just over a minute left, and J-Dub secured the rebound. Gil Goose got the ball, and he used a pick-and-roll to create space for a step-back 3-pointer. The shot went in. Aaron Gordon missed the next Nuggets shot, a contested corner 3 with 25 seconds left. Gil Goose was then fouled, and he made his free throws to put OKC up 111-103 with 22 seconds left.

The Thunder escaped this close contest with a win because Denver's thin supporting cast played so poorly. Jamal Murray shot 10-of-27, Russ went 1-of-7, Christian Braun was 3-of-12, and Micheal Porter was 1-for-7. By contrast, the Thunder spread their offense around. Six Thunder players scored in double-figures, led by Gil Goose with 31 points. J-Dub had 18 points and 9 rebounds, but he struggled again with his shooting, only making 5-of-14.

9 wins to go.

Game 6 in Denver. Loss vs Nuggets 107-119.

OKC had a chance to end the series, and they played well in the first half, taking a 3-point lead at halftime. However, J-Dub had his third straight game of terrible shooting (3-of-16), and Julian Strawther (!) came off the Nuggets bench to spark Denver to a home win.

Julian Strawther scored a quick 8 points with 3 minutes left in the 3rd quarter to put the Nuggets up 82-90. Strawther's hot streak continued in the 4th quarter, and he ended up hitting 3-of-4 3-point attempts while scoring 15 points in just 20 minutes. Strawther had only played 34 total minutes in the first five games, and 14 of those minutes came in garbage time of the Game 2 blowout. Strawther had been a complete afterthought by his coach, but he came up huge for Denver in Game 6.

Oklahoma City had clobbered Denver in the 4th quarters of the previous two games, 63-37. However, they could never pull close in this one. Denver and Strawther pressed their lead up to 14 points in the 4th quarter, and they kept it there.

Jamal Murray was sick with the flu, but he still managed 25 points, 8 rebounds, and 7 assists. Jokic had 29 points, 14 rebounds, and 8 assists, while J-Dub only scored 6 points for OKC. He was now 10-for-43 the last 3 games (he deserved a pass, though, as the Thunder would reveal after the season he was playing with a torn ligament in his shooting hand).

Brad texted out, "Never seen this Thunder team shoot so poorly from 3 going on 3 games in a row (OKC was 33-of-110)." I replied, "All wide-open 3's too. And J-Dub missed 3 layups. WTH?" Jeff said, "Great teams win Game 7's. We'll see."

The biggest news of Game 6 happened at the very end, when Aaron Gordon pulled his hamstring. Any athlete could see he would be severely limited in Game 7, although he would obviously try to play. But the next wrong move on that leg would end his season. Injuries like that would take weeks to heal. But Gordon only had three days until the two teams squared off for a final time. Denver already was very shorthanded. Who would play for them now?

Game 7 in OKC. Win vs Nuggets 125-93.

"Winning championships is so damn hard. This Nuggets team just won't die. They barely have anything left, though.", I texted before the game. Brad invited me to attend with him, and the arena was rocking. O-K-C! De-Fence! De-Fence! Denver actually started the game hot, jumping out to a 21-10 lead and quieting the anxious crowd. The Thunder's defense then started suffocating the Nuggets as OKC began a 50-25 run, and the crowd went crazy again. Jokic had dominated every defense that had been thrown at him this series. Coach Daigneault had finally put Alex Caruso on him at the end of Game 6 in frustration. It had worked. Caruso was given the assignment once again in Game 7, and he hounded Jokic, who ended up with only 20 points on the night.

The rest of his teammates didn't have enough left to give, either. The Denver starters missed 21 of their 26 3-point attempts, while OKC had 16 steals for 23 total turnovers (OKC's 74 steals were the most steals in an NBA playoff series in at least 30 years).

The game turned for good in the last five minutes of the first half, with OKC up 38-35. Aaron Gordon had been playing hard despite his injury. But as he went up to dunk the basketball, Gil Goose held him down to prevent the easy shot. The pressure of lifting two people off the ground, both Goose and himself, completely ruined Gordon's hamstring. He made his free throws to cut the lead to one, but he was really hurt now, and the Thunder took advantage. Chet had a dunk, then J-Dub hit a 3. J-Dub also scored on a breakaway dunk. Gil Goose made a 3-pointer, and J-Dub grabbed a steal for another breakaway dunk. Finally, Caruso stole the ball, leading to a J-Dub fast-break lay-up. J-Dub ended the half with a pull-up jump shot, and the Thunder lead had exploded from 1 point to 14. Jokic would soon be freed from his basketball responsibilities to go play with his horsies in Europe for the summer.

Denver didn't have the energy needed from their starters or enough talent on their bench to fight back in the 2nd half. The Thunder kept poring it on. Cason Wallace outran Jokic down the court and massively dunked over him with 6:30 to go in the 3rd. It sent us all into delirium. Denver finally threw in the towel only 2 minutes into the 4th quarter. Jokic dribbled up the court, and Caruso straight swiped the ball from him at halfcourt. Caruso went the other way, and he dropped the ball back for Goose to dunk, putting OKC up by 32 points. Jokic watched, dejected. Denver called timeout and emptied their bench. Some guy named Tyson started playing for them. Gil Goose had shot 12-of-19 for 35 points to lead the way. J-Dub went 10-of-17 for 24 points, including 11 points that broke Denver at the end of the 1st half.

With 7:40 left, the Thunder called their own timeout, and the crowd roared as the Thunder starters went to the bench with smiles on their faces. The series had been rough, but OKC had played a perfectly for a huge Game 5 win, and they blew Denver out of the building in Game 7. The Thunder had faced adversity, but had come out on top. We knew they could win it all.

8 wins to go.

Time for a quick check-in with the Eastern Conference. In the East, the teams had more varied records, unlike in the West. Cleveland had a standout season with 64 wins, while the defending champion Celtics had coasted to 61 wins. The Knicks had won 51 games for 3rd, while Indiana was sneaky good with 50 wins. A broken Milwaukee team ended with 48 wins. Meanwhile, a young Detroit team was much-improved with 44 wins, finishing 6th. Disappointingly, Orlando managed just 41 wins. Finally, Miami had a losing record, but they still managed to make the playoffs.

In the first round, there were no surprises. The Celtics beat Orlando 4-1. The Cavs swept Miami 4-0. The Knicks edged out Detroit 4-2. And the Pacers took down the Bucks 4-1.

The 2nd round got really interesting, though. New York ended the Celtics' title defense. The Knicks won the first two games in Boston. Then, they split the games in NYC. They lost Game 5 back in Boston, but Jason Tatum tore his Achilles tendon. Finally, they won Game 6 in a blowout at Madison Square Garden.

Even more surprisingly, the Indiana Pacers smoked the juggernaut Cleveland Cavaliers in just 5 games. And just like that, the two biggest threats to the Thunder had been eliminated, and the path to the championship had been cleared. The second and third seeds had been eliminated in the West, and the first and second seeds were gone in the East. OKC had no formidable teams left in their way. OKC couldn't possibly have hoped for a better outcome.

The Thunder's glory years of KD and Russ from 2012-2016 were littered with elite teams in the playoffs. The championship years of the Miami Heat of LeBron and Dwyane Wade were followed by the dominant Cavs of LeBron and Kyrie Irving. The Golden State Warriors ascended to win the title in 2015, and their 2016 team won an NBA record 73 games. And the Spurs were outstanding during that entire 5-year period as well, getting to the Final Four every year on average (they won 10 playoff series during that time, including a championship). The Thunder had great teams during those years, but there were always other teams just as good as them every one of those seasons.

2016 was the year that the Thunder were in their best position to win a championship. They had finally avoided injuries to their star players for the first time in four years. But they still had to beat a 67-win San Antonio team in the 2nd round, before facing the 73-win Golden State team in the Final Four (OKC lost in 7 games). And waiting in the Finals was LeBron at his apex. It was an almost impossible task.

By comparison, 2025 was a cakewalk for OKC. 51-win New York, 50-win Indiana, and 49-win Minnesota were the only other teams still remaining. Please already. Oklahoma City had better win the title. They could never have it this easy again.

The Western Conference Finals

The Minnesota Timberwolves were waiting for OKC in Round 3. Minnesota had experienced a similar trajectory as Oklahoma City over the past five years. Their ascent started when they drafted their star player, Anthony Edwards, with the number one pick in 2020. His rookie year of 2021 was rough, and Minnesota finished just one game better than OKC with 23 wins. Oklahoma City was still purposely losing in 2022, but Minnesota improved that year to 46 wins. The Wolves then won their play-in game against the Clippers to advance to the playoffs, but they lost in the first round to Memphis.

That summer the Wolves went all-in on their squad by trading for Rudy Gobert. They gave up Walker Kessler, four 1st round picks, and a pick swap to get him. Gobert's big contract pushed the Wolves' payroll into one of the most expensive in the league.

The initial results didn't go as well as they hoped. Minnesota struggled to integrate their players during the 2023 season, and they ended up winning just 42 games. Minnesota then beat the 40-win Thunder in the play-in to advance to the playoffs. They lost in the first round again, this time to the Denver Nuggets.

Both Minnesota and Oklahoma City made big leaps in 2024. They battled with each other and Denver until the final day of the season for first place in the West. The Thunder ended up winning 57 games, but they lost to Dallas in the second round. Minnesota won 56 games and made it to the Final Four, before they also fell to Dallas.

Unsatisfied, the Wolves again made a huge trade last summer, sending former number one pick Karlton to the Knicks for Julius Randle. The trade would help ease Minnesota's future payroll issues. It also solved the problem of Karlton's incompatibility with Gobert, as well as Karlton's lack of defense. The Wolves once again had trouble gelling, though. They finished in 6th place with just 49 wins, while the Thunder took another huge leap forward to 68 wins. However, after starting the season with a mediocre 31-27 record, Minnesota finished the season 18-6, and avoided the play-in games.

The Timberwolves were very talented despite their record. Minnesota was led by Anthony Edwards, an extremely athletic guard known for his explosive dunks. Edwards also shot over ten 3-pointers a night, 2nd only to Steph Curry in attempts per game. Rudy Gobert was their 4-time NBA Defensive Player of the Year center. Julius Randle provided secondary scoring at power forward. Another key player from Minnesota was SGA's actual cousin, Nickeil Alexander-Walker. I shortened his ridiculous name to Cousin of Goose.

They had played the Thunder tough during the season, splitting the four games with two wins each. Now they had made it to the Conference Finals again, after defeating the old lions LeBron James and Steph Curry in the previous two playoff rounds. They had sent the old, broken Lakers and the old, broken Warriors packing in just 10 games total. Well, good luck with the Thunder. They were in no way old nor broken.

Game 1 in OKC. Win vs Wolves 114-88.

The Wolves weren't prepared for the ferocity of the Thunder defense. The game was close until the 3rd quarter, and the Wolves led at halftime by 4 points with Gil Goose shooting 2-of-13. But the Thunder had 13 steals in the game, and they held Edwards to 5-of-13 shooting for 18 points. Edwards' teammates Naz Reid, DiVincenzo, and Cousin of Goose combined to shoot 7-of-36.

Julius Randle tried to keep Minnesota in the game, hitting 5 of his 6 3's for 28 points. After Mike

Conley hit a 3 to take a 56-60 lead midway through the 3rd quarter, the Thunder went on a 10-0 run to take the lead back, 66-60. Kenrich then hit a jumper and a 3-pointer on back-to-back plays to push the Thunder lead to 9 points. The teams spent the next 9 minutes answering each other back and forth, with the Thunder keeping the lead at around 9 points. Gil Goose and J-Dub drove to the hoop at will.

The Thunder started pulling away for good with 5 minutes left in the game, as Gil Goose hit a jumper to make it 96-84. With 4:30 left Goose was doubled, and he passed it to J-Dub, who swung it to Dort in the corner for an open 3-pointer to make it 99-84. Julius Randle drove in for 2 points on the next possession for 99-86. Goose was then doubled up top again with 4 minutes left, and he passed to Cason, who faked a pass to Dort in the corner, burning two defenders. Cason drove in, and help came over, so Cason laid up a crushing alley-oop for J-Dub to make it 101-86. Alex Caruso put the final dagger in with 3:06 left, hitting a 3-pointer for an 18-point lead. Dort stole the ball from Minnesota on the next possession, and the game was over.

J-Dub finished with 19 points, 8 rebounds, and 5 steals. Gil Goose rebounded from a bad first half to go 8-for-14 in the 2nd half, and he ended up with 31 points and 9 assists. The Thunder made 11 of their 21 3's, and they outscored Minnesota in the paint by a huge margin of 54-20. OKC dominated the 2nd half 70 to 40.

7 wins to go.

Game 2 in OKC. Win vs Wolves 118-103.

Oklahoma City won again at home. Their defense harassed Minnesota's stars into missed shots, while Gil Goose took over on the offensive end. Minnesota played zone defense for much of the game, but it wasn't nearly as effective as Denver's zone had been. Oklahoma City only shot 1-of-8 on 3's in the 1st quarter, but still led the game even though Minnesota had shot 5-of-11 on their 3's. OKC then took a halftime lead of 8 points thanks to Gil Goose scoring 5 points in the final 16 seconds.

The Thunder led 68-63 midway through the 3rd quarter, but they took control as Gil Goose led OKC on a 25-8 run to enter the 4th. Goose started the run by making a driving layup. Then Dort stole a pass, leading to Gil Goose driving in for a jump shot from the free throw line while getting fouled. 73-64. With 3:42 left in the quarter, Goose hit a pull-up jumper. Goose was doubled up top on the next possession, so he passed inside to Caruso, who passed out to Cason for a 3-pointer. 80-65. With 3:15 to go, Goose stole an entry pass to Gobert and put Cason on a fast break, and Cason laid up an alley-oop for Chet to slam home. 82-65. With 1:44 left, Cason drove to the basket, then dropped the ball to Chet for another dunk. 88-69. Naz Reid turned the ball over with 58 seconds left in the 3rd, and Goose then kicked the ball to Cason in the corner for a 3-pointer. The score was 93-69, and the Thunder lead had expanded to 24 points.

The Thunder kept the lead bouncing around 15-points for most of the 4th quarter. The score was 105-94 with 3:50 left, and the ball ricocheted down the court off a missed 3 from Dort. The Wolves tried to turn the long rebound into a fastbreak and get the game to single digits. However, J-Dub stepped in to steal the pass when McDaniels tried to drop the ball to Edwards. This sent the Thunder on a break in the other direction. J-Dub got the ball to Chet underneath the basket, but his dunk attempt was blocked by Naz Reid. J-Dub came flying in, rebounded the loose ball, and laid it in while being fouled.

The Wolves cut the lead to 10 points at 107-97 with 2:47 left. Dort then drove in and dropped the ball to Chet for a lay-up. Minnesota scored 2 points, then they doubled Gil Goose on the next possession, but he passed to J-Dub for a 3. Gil Goose then scored a contested lay-up on the following possession. This pushed the lead back out to 15 and finished Minnesota off.

Anthony Edwards had 32 points and 9 rebounds, but he was just 1-of-9 on 3's. Coach

Daigneault had shortened his lineup to 8 players, with Caruso, Cason, and Wiggins playing off the bench. J-Dub had 26 points and 10 rebounds, and Gil Goose dominated with 38 points and 8 assists. Oklahoma City had handled Minnesota at home pretty easily. On to the Great White North with a two game to nothing advantage.

6 wins to go.

Game 3 in Minnesota. Loss vs Wolves 101-143.

Minnesota destroyed the Thunder in Game 3. They did whatever they wanted to in the 1st quarter, with wide-open 3-pointers, easy drives to the basket, and sloppy turnovers from OKC. It was a really good impersonation by Minnesota of how the Thunder usually play. The Wolves led 41-72 at halftime, as the Thunder shot just 30% from the field in the first half. I texted out, "Jay quit at halftime. I can't finish the 3rd quarter." It was late, and I went to bed.

Minnesota hit 20 of their 40 3-point attempts, with Anthony Edwards going 5-of-8 and finishing with 30 points and 9 rebounds. Julius Randle added 24 points, and Terrance Shannon had 15 points in 13 minutes. The Thunder starters barely played half of the game, and Goose finished 4-of-13 for just 14 points. It was his lowest scoring game of the entire year. To sum up how poorly the game went, Dillon Jones ended up with 10 points for the Thunder. It was only the 8th "bad" loss of the year for Oklahoma City, but the playoffs weren't the time to suffer bad losses.

Game 4 in Minnesota. Win vs Wolves 128-126.

Game 4 was a must-win for the Wolves, but the Thunder was just too tough. OKC's star players showed out, and the Wolves' stars struggled. Anthony Edwards was 5-of-13 for just 16 points, and Julius Randle was 1-of-7 for 5 points, while OKC forced 23 turnovers and had 14 steals. Amazingly, OKC trailed in the game for only 36 seconds, despite how close the score was all the way to the end.

The Thunder lead was down to 4 points with 3:40 left, and OKC had possession for a huge play. Gil Goose worked a switch to get onto Gobert, and he was probing for an opening to drive. He slipped at the free throw line as help came over, fell to the ground, and lost the ball. Goose then somehow re-collected the ball as the Wolves surged in. He threw an unlikely nutmeg pass through McDaniels' legs from the ground to J-Dub. J-Dub then hit a wide-open 3-pointer, making the score 116-109.

With 2 minutes left, the Thunder had possession and the lead, 118-114. J-Dub had the ball at midcourt, with DiVincenzo guarding him. J-Dub ran the shot clock down to 12 seconds. He drove in to the left corner of the free throw line, pulling up from one of his favorite spots to shoot, and scored. This gave his team a 6-point lead. Cousin of Goose then missed a 3-pointer in the corner for Minnesota. DiVincenzo rebounded the shot and kicked it back to McDaniels, who passed to Cousin of Goose. He faked a shot before driving around a closing Gil Goose. Cousin of Goose made a tough bank shot over Chet, and he brought the lead back down to 4 points.

With a 1:25 left to play, Gil Goose slowly advanced from midcourt. The defense shaded towards him, and he snapped a pass to a wide-open J-Dub on the left side. J-Dub made the quick 3, pushing the lead to 123-116. The Thunder doubled Edwards on the next play, so he swung it to Cousin of Goose, who passed to McDaniels for a drive and an easy layup. 123-118. With 46 seconds left, Caruso was hounding Edwards. Edwards passed to McDaniels to drive in on Chet, but Holmgren stuffed his layup attempt.

McDaniels stole the ball from Goose on the next possession, leading to an Edwards missed 3-pointer. However, Cousin of Goose gathered the offensive rebound, and he passed the ball to McDaniels for a wide-open corner 3 with 24 seconds left. 123-121.

It took Minnesota a full 10 seconds to foul after the Thunder inbounded the ball for some reason.

They finally put Gil Goose at the line. Goose made both free throws, and Minnesota only had 14 seconds left. Rudy Gobert followed up a missed layup with two putback attempts, and the second one went in. Gil Goose was then fouled for two more free throws, but he missed the second one.

Minnesota was down by 3. The Thunder purposely fouled Naz Reid with 7 seconds left, and he made both free throws. 126-125. Gil Goose was then fouled and made both of his shots with 6 seconds left. 128-125.

Minnesota was out of timeouts, so they had to dribble the ball up from the backcourt. Caruso fouled Anthony Edwards as he crossed half line with 3 seconds left. Edwards made the first shot and then missed the second on purpose. The ball caromed sideways, and Goose gathered it in as he fell to the ground in the corner. He wisely launched the ball down the court before he could get fouled, but the ball went out of bounds just before time expired. The Thunder was only up by 2 points, but Edwards' desperation inbounds pass was easily intercepted to end the game.

Minnesota got strong play from their role players. Cousin of Goose and DiVincenzo shot 10-of-16 from three, scoring 44 points combined. McDaniels added 22 points, and Shannon had 9 points in 8 minutes. The Thunder only heavily used

6 players, as Hartenstein played just 16 minutes, and Wiggins didn't play at all. J-Dub went 6-of-9 from 3, scoring 34 points with 3 steals. Chet shot 9-of-14 for 21 points, and Gil Goose bounced back from his bad performance with a monster game of 40 points, 9 rebounds, and 10 assists.

Game 4 was such a great Thunder win. The series was headed back to Oklahoma City with the Thunder up 3 games to 1. OKC had 7 wins and only 1 loss at home in the playoffs, with an average winning margin of over 27 points. Good luck to the Wolves.

5 wins to go.

Game 5 in OKC. Win vs Minnesota 124-94.

"Send these fools to Cancun," I texted before once again heading down the Turner Turnpike to witness the game in person. It was a joyous night. The Thunder throttled Minnesota 26-9 in the 1st quarter, with 3 dunks and 2 layups to start the game, while the Wolves missed 17 of their first 20 shots.

Minnesota's malaise continued into the 2nd quarter. They began the game by shooting 5-for-18 from 3-point attempts. They also committed 14 turnovers in the 1st half. The game was over by halftime. The OKC lead was only 65-32, and Brad certainly wasn't ready to let his guard down, but I had no doubts.

My confidence had been cemented with 3 minutes left in the first half and the score at 55-27, as a Gil Goose layup was blocked by Anthony Edwards. This turned into a fast break for Minnesota, but Caruso stole the ball back from them underneath the Thunder basket. As the ball went the other direction on an OKC fast break, I noticed two Wolves players still standing under the Thunder basket. They never attempted to cross the free throw line, much less halfcourt. Their heart wasn't in it. They were already on vacation. It was over.

The Thunder forced 21 turnovers and grabbed 14 steals, and I would guess they scored 75 points in the paint? (It was actually 54 paint points). Minnesota's coach threw in the towel on their season early in the 4th quarter. Oklahoma City then emptied its bench with 5:14 remaining. Our star players danced their way to the sideline as the crowd roared. We loved these guys, and now they're headed to the Finals!

Gil Goose finished with 34 points, 7 rebounds, and 8 assists, and the Thunder starters shot 52% from the field. Hartenstein provided 2 blocks and 2 steals, Chet had 3 blocks, and Caruso had 4 steals. Isaiah Joe scored a quick 11 points in the last minutes of garbage time, making us laugh about the gambling implications. It had been a big party the whole game.

The whole crowd stayed afterwards to watch OKC get their meaningless Western Conference trophy. We showered the team with cheers. Coach Daigneault was interviewed for the crowd, and he said about his team, "They do everything right. They're professional. They're high character," and paused his answer as we drowned him out with our roaring approval. The players began draping their coach's shoulders with towels, towel after towel, just a ridiculous number of towels. Coach Daigneault finally got annoyed, and said with a smile, "They're idiots." This team was the absolute best.

4 wins to go.

The 2025 NBA Finals

I was not a Pacers expert, but I came to find out during a tense two weeks in June 2025 that they were an outstanding team. They played very hard individual defense with no weak links, and they were also very good at covering for each other defensively. They had big, tough players with long arms that created turnovers. Offensively, they did not play isolation hero-ball. They shared the ball until they generated an open look. The Pacers were confident that their athleticism and team defense would match up favorably with OKC, and they knew that their offense was humming.

The Pacers also had an excellent head coach in Rick Carlisle. Indiana was never out of games, were impossible to kill off, and never gave up. As my brother observed in the Finals, they played more like the Thunder than anybody else. This was the highest compliment we could give to an NBA team.

Why did a team this good not win very many games this season? (their record was 50-32). Once again, I wasn't a Pacers expert, so I wasn't sure. But they had an average year overall because they really sucked for the first half of the season. Indiana's record was just 18-18 on January 5th. The Thunder were 30-5 at that time, and OKC only lost 14 games all year. But the Pacers exploded to a 32-14 record from there, pretty close to OKC's record of 38-9 over the same stretch. Why such a poor start? I don't know. This isn't a book about the Pacers.

Indiana ran straight through the Eastern Conference in the playoffs. First, they beat the Milwaukee Bucks 4 games to 1, despite Johnny Boy averaging 33 points and 15 rebounds a game. And Milwaukee was up by 7 points with 40 seconds left in overtime in Game 5, but Indiana still found a way to win.

Next up was the 64-win Cavaliers. Indiana won the first 2 games in Cleveland, including Game 2 after being down by 7 points with 48 seconds left. Just like in the Milwaukee Game 5, Tyrese Haliburton hit the game-winning buzzer beater. Indiana finished off the 1-seed Cavs in just 5 games.

New York awaited in the semis. Haliburton sent Game 1 into overtime with a game-tying buzzer beater, and Indiana won both Game 1 and 2 in Madison Square Garden. The Pacers ended up beating the 3-seed Knicks 4 games to 2.

*****

How did Indiana acquire their 8-man rotation? Their best player was Tyrese Haliburton, whom they had acquired in a trade with the Kings for Domantas Sabonis. The Sacramento Kings drafted Haliburton with the 12th pick in 2020, adding the point guard to the young franchise point guard they already had in De'Aaron Fox. They soon gave Fox a huge contract extension, just months after drafting Haliburton.

The Kings then used the 9th pick in the next draft to choose Davion Mitchell, another point guard to add to their point guard collection. Haliburton had quickly proven himself to be a playmaking talent, but he was positioned as an off-guard in Sacramento. Haliburton had the body of a wing player, as he was 6'5" with very long arms. Much like Josh Giddey with the Thunder, Haliburton would never realize his potential as an off-the-ball player. He needed to run an offense himself.

With their point guard ranks overflowing, and their future pledged to Fox, the Kings now had a dilemma to solve. Indiana saw Haliburton's potential too, and offered Sabonis for him at the trade deadline in 2022.

Haliburton took off in Indiana in the three years since the trade. He was very tall for a point guard, and used his length to bounce side-to-side, finding angles to attack. His height also helped him to get off his atrocious looking shot, which would otherwise be easily blocked. His shooting motion started in front of his face instead of above his head, about a full foot lower than a normal NBA shot. It was as if Haliburton had learned to shoot at age 5, while still too weak to heave the ball to the rim. He then kept shooting with that same motion for the rest of his life. It didn't matter. It was effective for him. He was a high-scoring playmaker, a double-double machine, and a lethal late-game killer. NBA fans loved him and his game. In 2023, he averaged 20 points and 10 assists per game, and he was an All-Star for the first time. In 2024, he again averaged 20 points a game while leading the league in assists, and he was named to the All-NBA 3rd team. In 2025, his numbers were down slightly, but his importance hadn't diminished. Haliburton was named to the All-NBA 3rd team for the second season running.

The Pacers had found team success as Haliburton rose as a player. The Pacers were bad in 2023, finishing in 11th place, and well out of the playoffs. The next year they shockingly made the Final of the NBA Cup, and finished the season with 47 wins and the 6-seed in the East. It became clear that seeding didn't matter to the Pacers after the playoffs started. They beat both the favored Bucks and the favored Knicks to make the Final Four in 2024, before running through the heavily favored Cavs and the favored Knicks again in 2025.

The next most important player on their team was Pascal Siakam, a tall African who didn't like playing basketball as a kid. He eventually proved himself in the NBA, and he had averaged over 20 points per game for six straight seasons. Siakam also earned two All-Star appearances and two All-NBA teams (one 2nd, one 3rd). In 2019, was one of the best players on the Toronto Raptors as they won an NBA championship.

The Toronto Raptors were tearing down the remains of their championship team by 2023. When Siakam became available in January of 2024, the Pacers pounced, trading three 1st round picks to get him. I remembered people panning the trade at the time because the Pacers were gambling away their future, despite not being any good. It turned out that adding Siakam would make them very good and very successful in short order.

Another starter the Pacers acquired in a trade was their top defender Aaron Nesmith, a 6'6", stout, bulldog of a player. On offense, he was usually limited to hiding out in the corner to shoot 3's. He was their Lu Dort impersonator on defense. Originally picked 14th by Boston in 2020, Nesmith had limited chances with the loaded, title-hunting Celtics during his first two years. That summer Boston gave Indiana a 1st round pick in a trade for Malcolm Brogdon, and Nesmith was thrown in, too. Within months, he had been moved into the Pacers' starting lineup.

The final two Indiana starters were both players that they had drafted. Myles Turner, their 7-foot center, was selected with the 11th pick in 2015. A very athletic big man, he had been an important part of their team for his entire career. He also had been much criticized for what he didn't do- he didn't post up, he didn't score a lot, and he didn't get a lot of rebounds. But he was very good at what he did do. He had led the league in blocks in two different years, and he was a tough and quick defender. He also was a great stretch big man, very capable at shooting long jump shots and 3-pointers.

Andrew Nembhard was drafted in the 2nd round with the 31st pick in 2022 after three years of college basketball. A 6'4" combo guard, he was smooth and capable on offense, and very tenacious on defense. He didn't light up the scoreboard, averaging just 10 points and 5 assists in 2025, but he was a dependable scorer when needed. Nembhard consistently made winning plays, and filled in whatever gaps the Pacers had on any given night.

Nembhard had been a starter for almost his entire three-year career. Indiana gave him a contract extension before the 2025 season that paid him almost $20 million per year. The Pacers were widely criticized for overpaying a role player, but Nembhard proved to be well worth the money.

Benedict Mathurin was the Pacers 6th man. An excellent athlete, the 6'6" wing player was named Pac 12 Player of the Year as a sophomore, and Indiana drafted him in 2022 with the 6th pick. Although he hadn't been able to crack the starting lineup regularly in his first three years, he was an important part of the team. Mathurin averaged almost 30 minutes per game while providing tough defense and explosive scoring.

TJ McConnell was a short white guy who went undrafted out of college, but he had now played ten years in the NBA. A point guard who consistently made good plays, he only averaged 18 minutes per game in 2025, but he made those minutes count. Undoubtedly a bench player, with only 22 starts in the past 5 years, McConnell still would dominate multiple games in this NBA Finals. I used to like this overachieving underdog a lot until he tried to be the ruiner of our Oklahoma City dreams. The Pacers signed him as a free agent in 2019 for only $7 million over two years. He was an absolute home run acquisition.

Obi Toppin was a 6'9" big man who might be the highest leaper in the league. Drafted by the Knicks in 2020 with the 8th pick after winning NCAA Player of the Year as a sophomore, Toppin struggled to find his place in New York with Julius Randle playing in front of him. The Pacers traded for him before the 2024 season, giving the Knicks two 2nd round picks in return.

The Pacers also sparingly used big men Tony Bradley and Thomas Bryant during the Finals. Before signing a couple of 10-day contracts with the Pacers at the end of the season, Bradley was playing for something called the College Park Skyhawks. Thomas Bryant was acquired by Indiana in December from the Miami Heat basically for free. I was very, very happy anytime either player saw the floor in the Finals.

*****

To summarize how Indiana got here, they executed a quick rebuild starting in 2019. It was very similar to the chart of how the Thunder built their roster.

2015

- Myles Turner (1st round, 11th pick)

2019

- TJ McConnell (Free Agent)

2022

- Tyrese Haliburton (Traded for Sabonis)
- Benedict Mathurin (1st round, 6th pick)
- Andrew Nembhard (2nd round, 31st pick)

2023

- Aaron Nesmith (Traded for Brogdon)

2024

- Pascal Siakam (Traded for three 1sts)
- Obi Toppin (Traded for two 2nds)

Indiana, like the Thunder, capitalized on players that other teams overlooked, such as Toppin, Nesmith, and McConnell. They made smart trades for Haliburton and Siakam. Plus, they scored big with a 2nd round pick in Andrew Nembhard.

The players had to buy in to the team's philosophy while also working hard to improve themselves to be this successful. Haliburton and Siakam were proven players, and Indiana had to give up a lot to trade for them. But equally important was acquiring contributors like McConnell, Nesmith, and Toppin that other NBA teams didn't want at all.

(Unfortunately, Indiana would also provide another lesson in 2025 for the Thunder- How quickly a great team can fall totally apart.)

*****

All of the evidence pointed to Oklahoma City beating Indiana for the title.

In NBA history, the teams that had won at least 65 regular season games almost always went on to win the NBA championship. 21 teams had attained that win total, and 15 of them had won the title as well. And those numbers were skewed by the 2009 season that had a 65-win Lakers team (champions) and the 66-win Cavaliers (not champions). Another odd season was 2016, which had a 67-win Spurs team and a 73-win Warriors team, but neither team won the championship. The title went to LeBron's 57-win Cavaliers that year (Oklahoma City had to play both the Spurs and the Warriors in the playoffs that season).

73 Wins. 2016 Golden State Warriors,
with MVP Steph Curry. Lost in Finals

72 Wins. 1996 Chicago Bulls,
with MVP Micheal Jordan. Champions.

69 Wins. 1997 Chicago Bulls,
with MVP Micheal Jordan. Champions.

69 Wins. 1972 Los Angeles Lakers,
with Wilt Chamberlain. Champions.

68 Wins. 1973 Boston Celtics,
with MVP Dave Cowens. Lost in Semis.

68 Wins. 1967 Philadelphia 76ers,
with MVP Wilt Chamberlain. Champions.

The 2025 Oklahoma City Thunder, with their MVP Gil Goose, had now joined this illustrious list with 68 wins. But would they finish their season like the 2016 Warriors or the 1973 Celtics, and fall short of the title? Or would OKC win the championship like the other teams on the list?

As for the Pacers, the last time a team below the 3-seed won a title was 30 years ago, and that team was the defending champion Houston Rockets. Before that Houston team, the last team below a 3-seed to win it all was the 1969 Boston Celtics, 56 years ago. Teams below a 3-seed had made it to the Finals many times. But if those teams weren't good enough to have a great regular season, they just weren't ever good enough to win the championship. So, 65-win teams almost always won the title, and 4-seeds never did. And Indiana was a 4-seed playing against a 68-win team.

Additionally, Oklahoma City had set the all-time best NBA mark with a 29-1 record against the Eastern Conference in 2025. And the Thunder also handily won both games against the Pacers in the regular season. OKC was 8-1 in the playoffs at home, with a point differential of an amazing +221. In Oklahoma City, they were destroying everyone by almost 25 points per game (and they would finish the playoffs with an NBA all-time record best home point differential of +259). And no team had ever won a championship after starting a season as poorly as Indiana did (10-15).

*****

The Thunder's playoff results depended on how well their defense played. When OKC held their opponent to under 110 points a game in the playoffs, their record was 14-1. If OKC gave up over 110 points, they were just 2-6. This was consistent with their regular season as well, as the Thunder was just 8-12 when their opponent scored 115 points or more. But when OKC held the other team below 115 points? The Thunder was nearly undefeated, with 60 wins and only 2 losses.

Indiana had their own dividing line of success in the 2025 playoffs. The Pacers were practically unbeatable, with a record of 12-1, when they had at least six players score in double-figures. When Indiana wasn't sharing the ball and didn't have players scoring from all over the court, their playoff record was a poor 3-7.

So, Indiana's strategy was clear. If they wanted to do the impossible and beat this historic Thunder team, the blueprint was to share the ball on offense and get their score over 115 points. But the Pacers had already beaten some really good teams in the playoffs, and Indiana had made a record number of comebacks and a career's worth of memorable finishes. They were ready for the challenge.

Game 1 in OKC. Loss vs Indiana 110-111.

The Thunder had regained my confidence after they easily casted Minnesota aside, and I had no respect for 4-seed Indiana, texting, "Don't be scared. The people in Indiana, that's who's scared. Bet the house! Thunder are bringing it home."

I went to Oklahoma City for the game, and the Paycom Center was rocking. O-K-C! Dee-Fense! The crowd was amped. And everything went great in the game, until it didn't.

Coach Daigneault had decided to play small against Indiana. Isaiah Hartenstein only played 17 minutes, and Chet played just 23 minutes, while Cason Wallace entered the starting lineup. OKC closed the crunch time minutes of both halves with a super-small lineup of Dort, Cason, Caruso, Goose, and J-Dub.

Rick Carlisle had Indiana pressure Gil Goose full-court. This forced him to use extra energy bringing the ball up, and aimed to disrupt the Thunder's halfcourt offense. The Thunder struggled in the first half, shooting just 37%. They compensated by going 7-of-18 from 3 and sneaking 12 steals, and OKC was ahead at halftime, 57-45.

Rick Carlisle gave his team a pep talk in the locker room, telling them "We can't dribble into a crowd against this team. We have 19 turnovers. But (OKC) only got 9 points (from those turnovers). Not the end of the world. We're right there."

The Thunder kept their lead through the 3rd quarter, and it was 85-76 at the beginning of the 4th. Oklahoma City pushed their lead to 13 points with 9:42 to go. J-Dub then intercepted an Indiana inbounds pass, and he took it in for an uncontested breakaway dunk. Rick Carlisle was forced to call a timeout to try to salvage the game as the crowd went mental.

The Pacers went on a 4-15 run after the timeout, with Myles Turner and Obi Toppin hitting two 3's each to put the score at 98-94 with 6:16 to go. With

OKC up 102-98, Gil Goose had the ball at the top of the key against Andrew Nembhard. Goose split Siakam's double-team to attack the rim. Haliburton and Nembhard both met Goose at the bucket, but Goose avoided them for a beautiful layup with 4:01 left.

OKC was up by 7 points with 3:24 left, and Coach Daigneault subbed Chet out for his small closing lineup. Indiana took advantage by outrebounding Oklahoma City 6 to 2 the rest of the way, including 2 offensive boards. With 1:38 left, and OKC up by 3 points, Nesmith dribbled in past Gil Goose, but his layup attempt was blocked at the rim by Dort. Goose went the other way by himself with Toppin backpedaling, and he laid the ball in over Toppin and Turner.

Goose had the ball again with 1:09 left and a 110-107 lead, and he dribbled past Nembhard to the left to go up for a layup, but his shot was blocked by Siakam. Nembhard then jacked up a step-back 3-pointer under pressure, and it barely hit the rim, but the ball dropped right to Siakam. He put the ball right back up and in for a one-point game. OKC ran the clock down to 26 seconds, then J-Dub dribbled in, slid to his right, and shot an off-balance jumper. It went off the backboard, and down off of the rim, and out. The ball ricocheted into the corner, and Siakam gathered it, but he was bumped out of bounds. OKC kept possession, and

Goose again ran the clock down, still holding the one-point lead. Goose dribbled left against Nembhard, spun back into the lane, and stepped back into an open jump shot that bounced high off the rim and out.

Indiana gathered the rebound and quickly got the ball to Haliburton. Oh no. Haliburton crossed half line with 6 seconds left. Cason picked him up on defense. Haliburton dribbled up the right side of the court, and started moving towards the basket. Cason was backpedaling, and Haliburton suddenly pulled up into a long jump shot from just inside the 3-point line. He buried it. Game over.

I never once thought OKC would lose until Haliburton got the ball on the move with just 6 seconds left. Oklahoma City had controlled the entire game, and Indiana had never led. The crowd was stunned. It had been a typically suffocating defense by the Thunder, but the Pacers wouldn't die. They kept fighting, they kept the game close, and they buried their chance at the end. Indiana was now 7-2 on the road in the playoffs. OKC could still win this championship, but Indiana was a legit competitor. It was going to be a dogfight the whole series.

Gil Goose finished with 38 points, but J-Dub shot just 6-of-19 for 17 points. Lu Dort had 5 3-pointers, 4 steals, and 2 blocks, while Caruso contributed 11 points, 6 rebounds, 3 steals, and 2 blocks. The Pacers had six players in double-figures, and Haliburton, Siakam, and Nesmith all had double-doubles.

Game 2 in OKC. Win vs Indiana 123-107.

I watched Game 2 on my couch at home. The three days off after the shocking defeat in Game 1 allowed me to get some perspective. OKC had only lost two games in a row twice this season. They would respond. They always did. They had dominated Game 1. I was confident OKC would win Game 2.

Coach Daigneault wisely made some adjustments. He ditched the super small lineup, and he also played Hartenstein and Chet together some. Hartenstein had played really well in his limited time in Game 1. Another change was making Caruso and J-Dub responsible with bringing the ball up the court so Goose could rest a bit.

The Thunder had a 19-2 run in the 2nd quarter that turned a 33-27 scoreline with 9:38 left into a 52-29 lead with 4:24 until halftime. Indiana had gone 1-for-7 with 2 stolen balls and 2 other turnovers during that time. The game would never get within single digits again.

The play of the game occurred with 6:51 left in the 3rd quarter, and the Thunder leading 71-56. Gil

Goose trapped Siakam against the sideline. Hartenstein immediately jumped out to double-team him. Siakam attempted to pass out, but Hartenstein swatted the ball up court. Hartenstein dove to corral the ball before it went out of bounds, then got the ball to Goose while still lying on the ground. Goose dribbled the ball up court. He passed it to Caruso in the corner, who swung it back to Goose, who swung it to J-Dub, who swung it to Dort, who swung it to Caruso in the opposite corner for a 3-pointer.

With 10:40 left in the game, the Thunder had a 19-point lead, 95-76. J-Dub missed a jumper, but Caruso fought for the rebound, and he was able to swat the ball backwards. Wiggins won a 50/50 ball at the 3-point line, and he pulled up for a shot that he missed. Cason outfought Myles Turner for the rebound, and he kicked it out to Wiggins for another 3-point attempt. It went in. This OKC team just wanted it bad, fighting hard even with a huge lead. With 2:42 left, Coach Daigneault subbed his stars out.

The Pacers had finally lost a playoff game with 7 players scoring in double-figures. Gil Goose had 34 points and 8 assists, Caruso had 20 points, and Wiggins had 5 3-pointers for 18 points.

On to Indianapolis. I still didn't feel great because OKC had lost Game 1. And the Thunder had dominated Game 2, but they couldn't push past a 20-point lead to kill the game. Indiana just refused to die. Plus, the Thunder had sucked in Game 3's in the playoffs. OKC was down by 29 points against Memphis, lost to Denver in overtime, and got blown out in Minnesota. My friends were betting heavily against the Thunder in Game 3. And for good reason.

3 wins to go.

Game 3 in Indiana. Loss vs Pacers 107-116.

The winner of an NBA Finals Game 3 also ended up winning the title 80% of the time in series that had been tied at 1 game each. This was bad news for the Thunder, after the Pacers beat them in Indianapolis to take the 2-1 lead. Indiana won thanks to a huge game from Benedict Mathurin, and the magic of stupid TJ McConnell.

The Thunder led 19-10 to start the game. Chet scored 13 points in the 1st quarter, while Lu Dort drained his first 3 3-pointers. On the first play of the 2nd quarter, TJ penetrated into the lane for Indiana, and he dropped the ball to Siakam for an easy layup. Cason then inbounded the ball, but TJ intercepted his pass, and he got the ball to Siakam for a wide-open 3. Siakam missed the shot, but TJ rebounded the ball and dropped it to an open Mathurin for a layup. McConnell had garnered 2 assists, an offensive rebound, and a steal in one passage of play, and within 3-and-a-half minutes Indiana had taken the lead back. And TJ kept producing the entire time he was on the court, finishing with 10 points, 5 assists, and 5 steals in just 15 minutes of play. As Brad texted, "McConnell is killing us."

The Pacers pushed their lead to 7 points midway through the 2nd quarter, but OKC brought it back to a tie with some beautiful drives by Gil Goose. TJ then ended the half by driving into the lane before pulling up. He buried a jump shot to lead OKC by 4 points at the break.

It was 70-72 with 7:34 left in the 3rd, and Goose was getting mauled by Nembhard and Turner while dribbling. He tried to sling the ball across the court with his left hand. Haliburton jumped the passing lane and cruised the other direction for an uncontested dunk. It was the type of turnover and fast break that OKC regularly forced other teams into, but never conceded.

This had been a very close game (15 ties), and somehow the Thunder fought their way into a 5-point lead heading into the 4th. With 8:38 left, Indiana missed a shot, but the rebound ricocheted to Nembhard, and he made a jumper. Caruso then inbounded straight to McConnell, who laid the ball in. An Indiana miss had turned into 4 points in 2 seconds.

With 5:58 left and down by just 1 point, 100-101, the Thunder struggled. Three of their next four shots were blocked. This helped the Pacers extend their lead to 100-107. With 5:37 left, Myles Turner had stuffed a layup attempt by Chet. With 1:56 left, Turner made an easy block on a Chet 3-pointer. Chet then tried to drive on Turner, and he couldn't even get the shot up. I didn't know if Turner blocked the shot or stole the ball, but he was toying with Holmgren.

The Thunder still had a chance to win after Nesmith missed a 3, but Goose missed a step back jumper with Siakam in his face. Siakam then leaked out for a fast break layup with 1:09 left to make it 104-112. In all, the Thunder had 5 shots blocked and 3 missed 3-pointers in the last 6 minutes of the game.

As I texted to the fellas, "The good news is that the Pacers played perfectly, and TJ and Mathurin will never play better."

The Thunder had finished an unbelievable 61-2 in the regular season when leading at the end of the 3rd quarter. And they were now a floundering 1-and-2 against Indiana in the Finals.

Oklahoma City had shortened their rotation down to 8 guys, but Wiggins only received 10 minutes. Chet ended up with 20 points and 10 rebounds, but he missed all 6 of his 3-point attempts. He had to play better. Haliburton had 22 points, 9 rebounds, and 11 assists, and Mathurin scored 27 points off the bench while shooting 9-for-12. Indiana had 13 steals and 11 blocks, with Myles Turner providing 5 of the blocks himself.

Game 4 couldn't matter more. The Thunder had to win. There was no way they could come all of the way back from 3-1 down. My nerves were at 100. I couldn't believe this glorious season was going to end like this against this stupid Indiana team.

Game 4 in Indiana. Win vs Pacers 111-104.

I watched this game at my lake house, with my kids noisily playing around me, and the Thunder frustrating me to no end. The Thunder didn't play like the Thunder, and OKC was way behind in the 3rd quarter. But my team won with a bunch of help from Benedict Mathurin.

Coach Daigneault went back to his regular starting lineup with Hartenstein over Cason. I had texted out, "What is going on with Hart? I swear he had a double-double almost every game he played this year. He barely plays now vs the Pacers. Coach Daigneault doesn't like that matchup for some reason."

The Pacers ended the first half on a 15-6 run to go up by 3 points at the break. Indiana pushed their lead to 76-86 with 2:08 left in the 3rd. They had a chance to go up by more, but the Pacers couldn't capitalize when the Thunder missed their next 2 shots and had a turnover. Indiana missed 3 shots and 2 free throws over that same period.

Oklahoma City then went on a 13-3 run to tie the score at 89-89, as OKC had 2 steals and the Pacers shot 1-of-7, including 5 missed 3-point attempts. The score was 91-91, 95-95, and then 97-97 with 4:38 left. The Thunder had less than 5 minutes to pull out a win and save their championship hopes.

Gil Goose, our MVP superstar, took over the game, leading the Thunder on a 16-7 run to finish the contest. Goose shot 3-for-3 from the field and 8-for-8 from the free throw line, and he scored 15 of OKC's final 16 points. The iconic play of the game happened with 2:25 left and the Thunder down by 1 point. Goose cleared out the left side of the court to take Nesmith on 1-v-1. Nesmith fell as Gil Goose drove, and he kicked into Goose's foot, knocking him off-balance. Goose immediately recovered his balance as Nesmith watched from the ground. He stepped back into a 14-foot jump shot on the baseline as Nembhard contested. The shot went in, and the Thunder took their first lead of the 2nd half, 104-103.

But OKC still might not have won if it weren't for Bendict Mathurin's meltdown. Mathurin entered the game with 44 seconds left, and the Thunder up, 105-

103. Gil Goose was at the line after he had put Nesmith in the air on a beautiful pump fake at the free throw line. Goose then 360'd right around Nesmith for an open look, and he was fouled from behind. His two free throws put the lead at 107-103.

Myles Turner side-stepped a flying Dort to set up an open 3-pointer with 27 seconds left, but he missed off the front of the rim. Mathurin and Chet dove for the deflected rebound. Mathurin gathered it, while Chet was called for a foul. Then, Mathurin missed both of his free throws. And as the Thunder tried to inbound the ball, Mathurin blatantly held J-Dub as he tried to curl out and accelerate towards Caruso. It was an unnecessary off-the-ball foul that gave OKC a technical free throw.

With the score now 108-103, Caruso inbounded again. Haliburton tipped his pass up in the air and right to Mathurin. He drove in for a layup, but he was fouled again by a soaring J-Dub. Mathurin then missed one of the two free throws to make the score 108-104 with 19 seconds left.

Finally, before the Thunder's next inbounds pass, Mathurin ran right into the back of SGA. Goose collapsed to the ground after the NFL-like tackle, and OKC earned another technical foul shot. Gil Goose was then fouled again after the ensuing inbounds pass, and he made both of those free throws, too. The score was 111-104, and the game was over. With the score at 107-103, Mathurin had gifted OKC 2 extra points, while going 1-of-4 from the free throw line himself. The Indiana arena was stunned into dead silence.

It was so frustrating, despite the win, to watch the Thunder go exclusively to isolation plays with either Gil Goose or J-Dub again and again in this game. Those two players shot 42 of the Thunder's 78 field goal attempts and 21 of the 38 free throw attempts. OKC only had 11 assists, which was the fewest assists by a winning team in the Finals since 1948. And Goose finished without an assist for the first time all season.

The Thunder also only shot 16 3-point attempts, after averaging 39 attempts per game in the regular season. And OKC only made 3 of those 3-point attempts- it was the fewest made 3-pointers in a Finals win since teams actually started shooting them in 2010.

Any playoff series had its highs and lows. There was a constant tension between changing what wasn't working versus keeping what got you there. OKC had changed a lot of their tactics. The Thunder had gone small in Game 1, and it didn't work. Hartenstein had been benched, and the Thunder bench rotation had been shortened to just 7 or 8 players. Finally, the players had thrown out the sharing offense that had been a hallmark of the team for years. The new plan allowed Goose and J-Dub to drive to the basket again and again, generating shots and free throws at the bucket. It worked out for OKC in the end when Goose went supernova.

I let it out to the guys. "Dammit what a gut-wrenching win. I don't even know how we did it. Indiana seemed the better team all game. I felt like we were playing against OKC. Every shot for us was tough, they always had open shots, and their pressure kept turning us over."

Indiana only had 5 players score in double-figures. Caruso had 20 points and 5 steals (the first time in NBA Finals history a player had 20 points and 5 steals in a game). It was also Caruso's 2nd 20-point game of the Finals, after he didn't score 20 points in a single game all season (another NBA Finals record). The second record wasn't exactly surprising, though- Caruso had been kept in bubble-wrap all season, waiting for the playoffs.

And I needed to change up my own routine. Even though the Thunder had won the game, I was miserable. But Brad and Jeff were ecstatic, having watched it at a packed Oklahoma City bar. No more watching the NBA Finals with my uninterested family and the annoying Doris Burke. I needed to be in a crowd of Thunder fans. But, luckily, the series was tied again.

2 wins to go.

Game 5 in OKC. Win vs Indiana 120-109.

Game 5's in tied series were must win by definition, in every sport. And especially so for the home team. And especially in the Finals. Any team good enough to make the Finals was usually too tough to beat twice in a row, especially on the road.

It had been a horrible basketball series thus far. Oklahoma City didn't look inevitable, and Indiana seemed to be the more confident team. But I was feeling good about the situation, happy even. I felt like Indiana had run their luck out.

My brother and I debated on where to watch the game, settling on an old standby Tulsa dive bar, Crawpappy's. It was an inspired pick. The place was packed with Thunder fans, but we got perfect seats at the bar, right in front of the tv's and the attentive bar staff. I had finally found a location to match the moment.

And what a game it was! The Thunder was humming in the 1st quarter, with beautiful play after beautiful play. OKC started the game with J-Dub taking a crossover dribble-drive into a left-handed pass to a cutting Hartenstein for a dunk. Two minutes into the game, Siakam lost his dribble against Hartenstein. Goose picked up the loose ball and took off the other direction, releasing J-Dub on the left to outsprint Nesmith to the basket for a dunk.

With 8:57 on the clock, Hartenstein returned the favor to J-Dub. After receiving the ball at the top of the key, he immediately dropped a pass to a cutting Williams for a layup. With 8:32 left, Siakam drove in on the right against Hartenstein, and he lost his dribble again. OKC took the turnover the other direction. The ball circulated around to Hartenstein, who was posted up on Nembhard with his back to the basket. Frankenstein threaded a perfect bounce pass to a cutting J-Dub for a monster 2-handed dunk to make it 15-12. Oklahoma City was dominating the early moments with multiple back-breaking plays. How was OKC only up by 3 points?

Indiana was staying in the game by shooting 5-of-6 from the field with 2 3-pointers, despite coughing up turnovers and fastbreaks. OKC kept the pressure up, with two beautiful, weaving, coast-to-coast drives by Gil Goose through the whole Indiana defense. 23-15.

Oklahoma City was ready to break out. Cason intercepted an entry pass to Siakam, and J-Dub launched a long pass downcourt to a sprinting Caruso for a fast break. But as Caruso went up for the layup, Mathurin flew in from out of nowhere for a block from behind.

OKC ended the 1st quarter with a Wiggins 3-pointer, then a Cason 3-pointer, followed by another Cason 3-pointer, to lead 32-22. Indiana had the last possession. TJ's turnaround jumper, contested and possibly tipped by Cason, airballed to Mathurin under the basket. Mathurin went up for an easy shot, but Holmgren flew in for the stuff. Get right out of town! The Crawpappy's crowd was electric.

J-Dub took the game over in the middle of the 2nd quarter. He had a monster-dunk, an and-one layup, plus two more free throws. When he hit a 3-pointer with 3:35 left in the half, the Thunder had a 16-point lead at 52-36. The Thunder finished their great first half with a 14-point advantage.

In the 3rd quarter, our series nemesis, Stupid TJ McConnell, took over for Indiana. He entered the game with 6:40 left and OKC up 71-59, and he went 6-of-8 with 2 assists, a steal, and a free throw. TJ's 3-point attempt with 27 seconds left would have made it a 3-point game, but he finally missed a shot. J-Dub then closed the quarter with a jump shot to extend the Thunder lead to 87-79.

The Thunder lead was 92-82 with 10:57 to go in the game when the Pacers launched a comeback. Some lowlights included Gil Goose inbounding a beautiful lob pass from the frontcourt back towards the OKC end, but not to a Thunder player. Instead, it went straight to Siakam for a breakaway dunk. Then, Goose drove all the way to the basket for a left-handed layup, but Siakam swatted it away. The ball bounced to Wiggins for a wide-open 3, but he missed that shot, too.

Indiana worked another possession into a corner 3-point attempt for Nembhard, and his miss was rebounded by a skying Siakam. Siakam passed it out to Thomas Bryant, then he got the ball right back to drill a contested 3-pointer. Boom. Indiana's quick 11-3 run had brought them to 95-93 with 8:30 left.

OKC had an 18-point lead in the 2nd quarter, and now the Pacers were within 2 points. Indiana had come back to win from 15 points down 5 (!) times already in these playoffs- were they about to do it again?

Oklahoma City responded. J-Dub drove in on the next possession for a layup, but he missed the shot. Hartenstein tried to tip the basketball back in, but he missed again. Cason got that offensive rebound, and passed the ball out to J-Dub, and he nailed a 3-pointer. Cason then picked up pressure on Nembhard, and Nembhard tried to pass out to a teammate who had cut away. Nembhard's errant pass went into his backcourt, and it was picked up by Cason for a massive breakaway dunk. OKC had quickly put their lead back to 100-93.

Haliburton hit two free throws with 6:48 left to bring the score to 103-97, but a J-Dub jumper was followed by another steal off of Nembhard. Gil Goose had jumped the passing lane, and he cruised with the ball on a fastbreak for an and-one layup. Goose then stole the ball from Haliburton, and assisted to J-Dub for a layup. This quick mini-burst made the score 110-97 with 5:48 left, and the game was over. The crowd was rocking, both at the bar in Tulsa and at the arena in Oklahoma City.

But don't take my word for it. Jalen Williams was asked about the Oklahoma City fans after the game. He said, "Very loud. Extremely loud. Feels like the court is shaking…It's just so loud here, it's deafening. Like I remember I was trying to yell a coverage to Lu before the play gets in and we're like two feet away and we can't hear each other."

The Thunder defense, their calling card all season long, was the story of the game. OKC's pressure had broken the Pacers in the 4th quarter for the second game in a row. Oklahoma City finished with 15 steals and 12 blocks (and the Thunder would finish the playoffs with an NBA record turnover differential of +131). Cason and Caruso had 4 steals each, and Gil Goose had 2 steals and 4 blocks. The Thunder outscored the Pacers off of turnovers 32-9.

Pascal Siakam led the Pacers with 28 points, and TJ had 18 points and 4 assists in just 22 minutes. However, Mathurin only shot 2-for-11, and Haliburton only scored 4 points on 0-for-6 shooting. Haliburton had pulled his calf muscle in the 1st quarter, and he was doubtful to play in Game 6. Of course he was going to try to play, though.

Gil Goose had 31 points and 10 assists for OKC, but J-Dub led the Thunder with the best game of his career. He was an unstoppable 14-for-25 for 40 points in the huge victory.

It was the best feeling! What a great win! This team was going to do it! And our bar tab after hours of drinking and eating was only $57! What a great day!

1 win to go.

Game 6 in Indiana. Loss to the Pacers 91-108.

The Thunder was going for the NBA title, and I had to be in Oklahoma City when they won. Tulsa was too far away- I wanted to be at ground zero for the celebration. I did not know what would happen, but after all these years, I couldn't miss it.

Well, the celebration sure didn't happen after Game 6.

Everything went wrong. It started when I set up shop at Social Capital, which was a fine bar within walking distance of Paycom Center. Social Capital also was the worst possible choice for watching a big game. It was too packed, at standing-room only, and any drink or food had to be ordered at the bar instead of through waitresses.

I was able to secure a seat at a picnic table through the kindness of a random family that had a little extra space. But the lines for the bar and the bathroom were so long that all my friends and I spent half the game waiting in queues. We were never at the table to watch the game together, not that there was anything to cheer.

With 5 minutes left in the 1st quarter, J-Dub tried an easy outlet pass to Caruso in the backcourt with no pressure on him. TJ somehow deflected the pass, grabbed the ball just before it bounced out of bounds, and passed it to Toppin for a 3-pointer.

With 4:40 left in the 2nd quarter, and the Thunder down by 10 points, Isaiah Joe tried to drop a pass along the sideline back to Lu Dort. Haliburton skied to tip it to Turner, got the ball back, and passed it to Siakam. Siakam passed it to Nesmith on the wing to nail a 3-pointer. A steal and 4 quick passes without a single dribble, finished with a 3 for a big lead. And on it went. The Pacers outscored the Thunder 17-36 in the 2nd quarter, and they had a 22-point halftime lead.

OKC scored 35 total points in the 2nd and 3rd quarters combined. I spent the entire 2nd quarter, halftime, and part of the 3rd sulking in a line that wrapped across the entire restaurant and out the front door. It was maddening to stand in line for an hour, trying to watch a faraway screen as our Thunder hopes slipped away. The game was already over by the time I got my pitcher of beer. Ben Sheppard then hit a long 3 to beat the buzzer at the end of the 3rd quarter. The Pacers were up by 30 points, and the bar started clearing out.

The OKC starters shot a combined 1-for-13 from 3, and Dort and Chet shot a combined 3-of-14 on their field goals. Indiana had 16 steals, while the Thunder only had 4! OKC committed 21 turnovers, and Indiana outscored OKC in fast break points 22-11.

Haliburton had been questionable to play with his strained calf. But he didn't look hampered at all, and he scored 14 points in 23 minutes. Indiana had 6 players in double-figures. TJ McConnell had yet another great game with 12 points, 9 rebounds, 6 assists, and 4 steals.

The less said about this terrible game, the better. I left before it ended to try to beat the traffic home.

One game left for all the marbles.

Game 7 in OKC. Win vs Indiana 103-91.

I didn't have tickets to the game, but I still wanted to be in Oklahoma City on a championship winning night. So, I headed right back down the Turner Turnpike a day after returning from the disappointment of Game 6. I wasn't really worried about the Thunder, though. It felt more like the day of an awesome concert had finally arrived after months of waiting- the anticipation was giving me some anxiety, but most likely it was going to be a really memorable night once the show started.

The media kept pointing out how similar both the Denver series and this Indiana series had been. Both of the Game 1's were miraculous losses in Oklahoma City on buzzer beating shots. Up 3 points with 11 seconds left vs Denver, Aaron Gordon had hit a 3-pointer to win. Up 3 points with under a minute left against Indiana, and Haliburton went the distance of the court for a buzzer-beater.

The Game 2's were both Thunder revenge games after those shocking home losses. The wins were huge blowouts by halftime. The Game 3's both were disappointing losses away from home. Trying to regain homecourt advantage, the Thunder were up in both games, but ended up losing both by 9 points each. OKC had even pushed the Denver game to overtime.

Those losses set up must-win Game 4's on the road for OKC, and both games could have gone either way. OKC was up by 5 points against Denver with 23 seconds left, and they still almost lost. Against Indiana, the Thunder went away from their identity, but won thanks to Gil Goose's excellence and Mathurin's implosion. Neither win left me feeling great. And both series had been way harder than what I thought they would or should be.

The Game 5's positively changed the sour mood of both series, as the Thunder proved they were the better team while going up 3 to 2. Although both games were close, the Thunder had maintained control throughout, and the results weren't in doubt in the final minutes.

Then the Game 6's happened, and the pressure was cranked back up on the Thunder. The Game 6 in Denver was close through 3 quarters, but the 4th quarter was all Nuggets. The Indiana Game 6 was a blowout from the start. And the Thunder had been huge road favorites in both games.

The Denver Game 7 was a Thunder blowout win. So, it would logically follow that the Pacers were in trouble. The Thunder also had the NBA's best ever winning percentage in games following a loss in the regular season and playoffs at .900 (18-2). And the game was in Oklahoma City. NBA home teams had a 15-4 record in Game 7's of the Finals. It only made sense that this would be the night we had waited 17 years for.

After the debacle two nights previous at Social Capital, I had to pick the right setup for Game 7. My friend Jeff rightly insisted that we start our day's adventure at the Oklahoma City staple Edna's Bar. One of Edna's famous Lunch Boxes would surely bring us luck. We then made our way downtown, and just outside of the parking lot we came across the soccer bar Skinny Slim's. We swung in for a drink, but that bar was too small for what I was after, plus all the seats were already taken. I knew what I wanted- a seat at a bar with a packed house and great service.

We were getting short of time, but I knew Rendezvous Pizza would be a great choice. The lobby was packed with people waiting for a table, and the bar was full as well. But a lot of people at the bar had tickets to the game, so I was able to quickly get a prime seat.

The beers were flowing. I was excited. The crowd was ready. I believed in this team. I knew the arena would be rocking. This team always responded to losses. It was tough playing against Indiana, but it was even tougher for them to play against OKC.

I can't start recapping Game 7 without first talking about Tyrese Haliburton. Haliburton had started Game 7 off hot, hitting three 3-pointers, and continuing his good play since his calf injury.

However, with 5:03 left in the 1st quarter, Haliburton received a pass at the top of the key with the shot clock running down. He started to drive by Gil Goose, and his foot slipped out. The bar started cheering as he fell to the floor. Haliburton's turnover led to an easy fastbreak layup to give OKC the lead. The cheering continued (but not by me) when the camera panned back to Haliburton still lying injured on the ground. But when the replay showed his Achilles tendon clearly snapping off of his heel, the whole place let out an "ohhhh" in sympathy, followed by silence. It was a graphic injury, and it was obvious that Indiana had lost their best player for the rest of the game. No one wanted that to happen. But I think the Pacers still would have lost Game 7 if Haliburton didn't get hurt.

Indiana didn't let Haliburton's injury stop them. They fought hard the entire 1st half, and the game was back and forth. There were 10 ties and 11 lead changes, as neither team could capitalize to take an advantage. Both teams were playing excellent basketball.

The Thunder came out to win in the 2nd half. Chet started the 3rd quarter with a layup, followed by the iconic play of the game. Lu Dort had the ball knocked free by Siakam with the shot clock almost expired. Lu gathered the ball from way behind the 3-point line and hurriedly launched an off-balance shot that somehow still swished in.

The Thunder had started the half with 5 quick points to lead 52-48. When Chet stuffed Mathurin's shot attempt on the Pacers' next possession, OKC was poised for yet another 3rd quarter run. But the Pacers never die. Siakam got the ball back after the blocked shot, and he made a timely 3-pointer to bring the score back to 52-51.

OKC continued their pressure, and a Caruso layup was followed by a steal that led to another layup by J-Dub. Indiana again killed the momentum with a 3-pointer from Myles Turner to tie the game back up at 56-56. Oklahoma City then really tried to break Indiana's confidence. OKC got a 3-pointer from Goose. J-Dub then stole the ball from TJ, which led to a 3-pointer from Chet. Dort followed with another steal from TJ. Finally, Goose orchestrated a beautiful, spinning drive that J-Dub finished with an open 3-pointer. This put the Thunder lead at 65-56 with 7:16 left in the 3rd. Rick Carlisle stopped the bleeding with a timeout. Surely this was the run that would put the game away.

But Indiana hung in the contest, and TJ took over for them. He scored all the Pacers' next 10 points with a series of tough drives and contested finishes at the rim. This kept the game close at 70-66 with

3:54 left. Jeff was beside himself, furious that nobody on the Thunder could stop TJ yet again. Calm down, Jeff. TJ couldn't guard anyone on OKC, and the Thunder was targeting his defense on every offensive play. And TJ can't keep making these impossible shots for the rest of the game.

Sure enough, OKC dominated the last few minutes of the 3rd quarter. With 2:50 left, Hartenstein and Caruso trapped TJ as he crossed half-line, forcing him into a turnover. Hartenstein picked up the ball and tossed a perfect pass over the defense to put Cason in for a fastbreak layup. The crowd knew the Pacers' breaking point was near, and they were going crazy. OKC swarmed Indiana while making 5 of their last 7 shots (plus one full-court heave at the buzzer), and entered the 4th quarter with a formidable 81-68 lead. Although Indiana kept blunting OKC's attempts to put the game away in the 3rd, Oklahoma City ended up outscoring the Pacers 34-20 in the quarter.

The Thunder extended their advantage at the beginning of the 4th quarter, as Indiana started the final 12 minutes of their season by missing 6 shots in a row with 2 turnovers. The Oklahoma City lead was 90-68, a 22-point advantage with just 7:41 left. The game was over.

But no, Indiana just refused to die. The Pacers started drawing fouls, and they went 7-for-8 from the line during an 11-1 run. This brought the score to 91-79 with 4:45 to go. Gil Goose then missed a 3-pointer with 3:52 left, giving Indiana a chance to get within single-digits. But TJ turned the ball over on the next two possessions with the championship on the line. Although both turnovers were followed by misses by Goose and J-Dub, Indiana now only had 2:47 left.

The bartender pulled his staff together in front of me. "No more drinks. Don't sell any, because I'm not pouring any more. Tab everyone out." Was he afraid of a riot? No one knew what to expect. I still had beer in my pitcher, so I'd be fine. Everyone was cheering. Jeff was still nervous. "The game's not over yet." Oh, Jeffrey, it was over.

Andrew Nembhard made a long 3-pointer over Chet with 2:31 left to make the score 94-84, but Chet leaked out behind the Pacers, and J-Dub found him with a full court pass for an easy dunk. It was a crushing blow. My eyes were full of tears. OKC did it! They actually did it! All these years of waiting. All the Thunder games I had watched. And now they were champions!

The restaurant was chanting OKC! OKC! OKC! Indiana wouldn't get the score within single-digits, as the Thunder made 8 of their last 10 free throws. The clock kept slowly ticking down. OKC put the final nail in the coffin with 1:20 left. Nembhard tried to dribble-penetrate past Dort at the 3-point line, and Lu knocked the ball away for a turnover. Indiana had finally been vanquished. High fives. Hugs with strangers.

The Thunder bench emptied as the OKC starters received their curtain call with 32 seconds left, embracing each other, a job well done. The crowd roared. Then the final buzzer. The long journey was over. Chet was hugging everybody. Gil Goose was playing it cool, as always. Caruso and Dort were jumping with excitement. J-Dub couldn't stop crying, hiding his eyes with the collar of his shirt.

Indiana only had 4 players in double-figures. Siakam was 5-for-13 for 16 points, but stupid TJ shot 8-for-13 for 16 points, and Mathurin had 24 points and 13 rebounds. Chet had 18 points and 8 rebounds, J-Dub had 20 points, and Gil Goose had 29 points and 12 assists, but shot just 8-of-27. J-Dub, Goose, and Dort combined to shoot just 6-for-28 from 3 (an abysmal 21%).

The Thunder had struggled on offense, but the defense, appropriately, had carried the day. The Thunder had 14 steals and 8 blocks, and they won the turnover battle 23 to 8. OKC outscored Indiana on points off of turnovers 32 to 10, including 18 points in the pivotal 3rd quarter. Chet dished out 5 blocks, which was the most blocks in a Finals game ever. OKC's 3-headed monster of Dort, Caruso, and

Cason had 3 steals each. And all the fast break points helped OKC to outscore Indiana in the paint, 40-26.

The action shifted to the stage for the trophy presentation. The crowd was on their feet and cheering. Sam Presti took the microphone. "Oklahoma has a true TEAM, and not just a winner." Coach Daigneault was next. "(these players) behave like champions. They compete like champions. They root for each other's success, which is rare in professional sports... They are an uncommon team, and now they're champions."

Lisa Salter called Chet to the microphone. She said, "You suffered that injury early in the season," ...and his response as he looked down, thinking about his words, was "Broken bones, bruises, it's all temporary" ... and as he raised his head up, looking at his home crowd with a smile, "But this is FOREVER! Let's go! ... It's going to be a great night in Oklahoma City!"

Alex Caruso was called up to the mic. "Sam (Presti). Clay (Bennett). They had the belief to bring me here to be part of something special. And special is what we were." Lisa Salter wrapped up the ESPN courtside broadcast, saying, "Once again, all of you... the 2025 NBA Champion Oklahoma City Thunder, It's your time, guys, celebrate." The crowd was deafening with their chant... OKC! OKC!

OKC!... as the team took championship photos on the stage together, with championship hats, and championship t-shirts, and the Larry O'Brien NBA Championship trophy. Doris Burke finished the broadcast by saying, "They were down in the Denver series, they were down in this (Indiana) series, and the maturity, the ability to play beyond their years..." as Gil Goose and J-Dub sat together, smiling, and taking pictures next to their trophy.

Gil Goose was interviewed postgame after being named MVP of the Finals. "Our togetherness on and off the court, how much fun we have...it made it so much easier. All the achievements and accolades don't even come close to the satisfaction of winning with your brothers. Feels amazing...so much weight off of my shoulders. I am just glad and happy that every one of my dreams came true." I was exploding with pride, sitting a half-mile away from these Oklahoma City heroes, but celebrating with them.

Rendezvous Pizza was mostly empty as the broadcast ended. The staff was cleaning up, and my beer was almost out. What to do? Oklahoma City really didn't know. We'd never won a championship. The last Finals game was 13 whole years ago.

We went down the stairs to the street level heat of summer. It was so hot, but our arms were raised in triumph. I had texted out, "About to lose my f***ing mind! We're going to ride that bronze buffalo statue in our tighty whities and do cannonballs into the Bricktown canal!"

The streets were teeming with people leaving the stadium and flowing towards their vehicles. OKC! OKC! OKC! How do you celebrate an NBA championship on a Sunday night, with work in the morning?

I stopped at a Bricktown street corner, and offered up my hand in "high-five" to the mass of people passing by. Everyone wanted one. We were bursting at the seams with happiness, and needed an outlet. One after another, high-five, high-five, high-five. Jeff left to find Brad. He wanted his celebratory hug with his best friend, two guys who had owned season tickets together for 14 years. I stayed behind. High-five. High-five. High-five. I was staying just clear of the moving mass of people on the sidewalk, but still causing traffic jams, as multiple people in each passing group paused to get their high-five.

One thousand high-fives later, and Jeff returned. He had gotten his hug. We were on the move again, but Bricktown was at a standstill, the streets packed with cars fighting their way home to the suburbs. We walked past the lines of sitting cars, around them and between them, and I offered my high-fives still. Windows rolled down. Drivers honked their horns. Passengers chanted "O-K-C" into the summer heat. Everyone wanted more. High-five. High-five. High-five. Groups of cops watched for the riots that of course wouldn't come. They wanted to be serious business, but I was drunk and delirious and idiotic. A smile and a high-five for the cops, too, but keep it moving. Same with the National Guard, and their machine guns and barricades. They had the wrong city. High-fives for them as well. Share in the joy.

It had been over an hour since I had entered the downtown Oklahoma City streets, and my high-five hand was bruised and sore. The roads were slowly clearing, but as we neared the parking lot that held Jeff's truck, Skinny Slim's soccer bar again appeared before us. It had been the first place downtown we had stopped hours previous. We had been nervous then, and apprehensive. Now, we were drenched in sweat and alcohol, and we had become world champions. Most every other bar and restaurant in Bricktown had long closed down for the night, but Skinny Slim's was still open, and it was packed with celebrating fans. Hundreds of people spilled outside onto the patio and into the street. We didn't ever want the night to end. We continued the celebration as long as we could.

*****

I had never equated the Oklahoma City Thunder with the Oklahoma City Bombing. The bombing happened thirty years ago, but I still cry when I think about it. I have never met a fellow native of the city who didn't know of someone that was murdered that day.

Sam Presti famously made every new Thunder player go to the Bombing Memorial when they first joined the team, before doing anything else. No exceptions. Nobody can understand Oklahoma City without witnessing what had happened.

The city hosted our victory parade two days after the Thunder won the NBA championship. Hundreds of thousands of citizens attended the celebration that Tuesday morning, including me and my 5-year-old son.

The following day I saw the most beautiful photograph I had ever seen. A Thunder bus traversing the parade route had passed in front of the Murrah Bombing Memorial, where the 168 lives had been stolen in 1995. The team bus was facing the camera, and it was framed by the cheering fans lining the streets around it. A banner that said "CHAMPIONS" hung across the top of the bus, and the Western Gate of the Memorial rose up in the background behind the bus. The Western Gate represented 9:03 AM, the minute after the bombing had happened, after which everything changed for all of us Oklahomans, forever.

And on top of the bus is Gil Goose, our hero, our MVP, with his back turned to the camera, facing the Memorial. His outraised hands seem to touch either side of the gate, in triumph and jubilation, reaching into the past, but having changed the city once again. Forever.

Epilogue: The Upcoming 2026 Season

The rich got richer. Oklahoma City had the best team in the NBA, and the whole team returns to defend their title. The 12 most important players for OKC- Goose, J-Dub, Chet, Cason, Dort, Hartenstein, Joe, Wiggins, Ajay, J-Will, Kenrich, and Caruso- are all back and signed to contracts, and the team was under the salary cap and both aprons. Additionally, the Thunder have added more talent to their championship roster with 3 rookies- Topic, Barnhizer, and Sorber- looking to break into the team. The Thunder will run into significant salary cap issues in 2027, but 2027 is a long way away.

(Roster update as the book goes to press- Thomas Sorber decided to join Chet Holmgren and Nikola Topic as recent 1st round picks who will miss their rookie year through injury. Sorber tore his ACL in a summer workout.)

The Thunder are so young that they should even be better in 2026 than they were in 2025. OKC is the clear title favorites. But another championship won't be easy. The rest of the NBA didn't stand still.

So, who will the other title contenders be in 2026?

Plenty of teams have title aspirations. But most of those teams won't be threats.

Boston and Indiana are out. Those two teams would have led the list of 2026 title contenders behind OKC, but their seasons were already ruined by the Achilles tears of star players Jason Tatum and Tyrese Haliburton.

The Lakers, Warriors, and Bucks are all too old. They didn't improve their teams enough in the offseason when they already weren't good enough to win in 2025.

The Clippers have amassed a lot of talent, but they are maybe the oldest NBA team ever. Their only players next season on the right side of 30 years-old will be the veterans Ivica Zubac and John Collins. I'm going to believe in the youth of the Thunder over the geriatrics of Los Angeles.

Memphis, Orlando, Dallas, and San Antonio all fancy themselves as rising contenders, but none of them have proven themselves in the playoffs yet. Memphis and San Antonio have skilled young players who might become superstars, but they are just as likely to miss the playoffs in 2026 as to make them. Dallas and Orlando have a lot of coalescing to do as teams to become actual title threats. I don't think Orlando has the offense to get it done. And Dallas' hopes rest on Kyrie Irving coming off an ACL tear and on Anthony Davis staying healthy.

To the fans of the Hawks and the Pistons, I tell you, "No." But what if the 76ers all get healthy?

Won't happen. The other bottom-tier NBA teams? Who cares?

But here are the 5 teams that will be roadblocks, obstacles, and problems...

5. Houston Rockets. 2-seed in the West last year with a very young team. They got rid of Jalen Green, which was positive. They also got rid of Dillon Brooks- not so positive. They are very big, and their defense should be great. Houston should improve, but they have a lot of question marks. Will they have enough shooting to be the best? And how will Durant fit in? It sure didn't work out for him in Brooklyn or in Phoenix.

Update as we go to press... Fred Van Vleet tore his ACL in September. The Rockets lost a star player, and their only good point guard. This will seriously dent their chances if they don't replace him.

4. Minnesota Timberwolves. They made the Final Four in each of the last 2 seasons, and Anthony Edwards still hasn't hit his prime. Minnesota could improve this season. But they lost an important player in Cousin of Goose, and they didn't add anyone new. Rudy Gobert is getting old, and Mike Conley is getting really old. And Minnesota already couldn't beat OKC.

3. New York Knicks. They are a really talented team, good at both offense and defense. They have a new coach who will play his guys less than 40 minutes a game- will some rest help them find another level? The Knicks improved their bench, too.

2. Cleveland Cavaliers. Cleveland is all-in on going for the championship. They are a really talented team that play winning basketball, and their whole team is basically returning. And the chip on their shoulder is the size of a boulder. Donovan Mitchell has had his doubters his entire career, and Cleveland badly flamed out of the playoffs in 2025 despite winning 64 games. They have everything to prove.

1. Denver Nuggets. I spent a fair bit of this book making fun of Denver's complete lack of a bench in 2025. Plus, some of their "big name" players don't live up to their huge contracts. Despite those debilitating deficiencies, Denver still almost beat OKC, thanks to Nikola Jokic. Well, this year they got Jokic some help coming. Cameron Johnson, Tim Hardaway, Bruce Brown, Jonus Valanciunas... it's just a huge step up from the players coming off the bench in 2025. Plus, Christian Braun is now a legit NBA starter, and Jamal Murray and Aaron Gordon already have championship chemistry with Jokic.

HOWEVER... The Oklahoma City Thunder is by far the favorites for the title in 2026. I can look at the teams above and make the case about how they will be contending teams. But if I were them, looking at Oklahoma City, how could I possibly expect to win? OKC is an unsolvable problem for the rest of the NBA. And it's all house money after the championship in 2025.

The 2025 season was so spectacular. The Thunder finished 3rd in offensive rating, 1st in defensive rating, and 1st in overall rating. Oklahoma City's record ended up being 84-21, for a winning percentage of .800. The only other championship teams in NBA history with at least 84 wins were the 1996 and 1997 Chicago Bulls.

The Thunder not only had lots of wins, but they won those games by big margins. OKC's games usually weren't close in 2025. They ended up with the best point differential in NBA history, scoring 1,247 more points than their opponents did. OKC lost 22 of their 105 games (with only 9 bad losses), and they won 20 "close" games. The Thunder also had an amazing 64 "big" double-digits wins, setting the NBA record for most wins by at least 10 points. An extraordinary 61% of the games the Thunder played in the 2025 season ended up with an easy OKC win.

OKC didn't slump into losing streaks, as they only had back-to-back losses two times in the regular season and the playoffs. OKC set an NBA record for best winning percentage in games following a loss at .905 (19-2). The Thunder destroyed the Eastern Conference, setting an NBA record by going 29-1. Their only loss to an Eastern Conference team was on the road in Cleveland, against a team on a 10-game win streak.

The Thunder actually destroyed almost every team in the NBA. The teams that gave them trouble during the regular season were Denver, Golden State, Minnesota, and Dallas (of course). OKC's record versus those four teams was 6 wins and 9 losses. Against the other 25 teams, the Thunder's record was 62-5!

And the Thunder team is still extremely young. Of the 14 most important players, only Caruso and Kenrich will turn over 30 years-old in 2026, and 7 of those players will be 25 years-old or younger. This team, for the most part, is either just beginning their primes or at the start of their careers. They should be even better in 2026. I can't wait...

About the Author

A native of Oklahoma for most of his life, Brian graduated from Putnam City High School in 1996. He then matriculated from Oklahoma City University in 2000, and followed with graduate school at the University of Oklahoma. Brian has lived in Tulsa since 2002. But the majority of his first 25 years were spent in Oklahoma City, where he watched the city transform itself.

For someone who has never played basketball, Brian will talk incessantly about the Thunder without prompting. Although his deep knowledge is suspect, his fandom is not. Brian has watched the Thunder and followed them closely for years.

Brian is blessed with a wife and two children.